GOOD MORNING. . . GOD

GOOD MORNING... GOD

Pamela Steinke

New Leaf 🍃 Press
P.O. BOX 311, GREEN FOREST, AR 72638

FIRST EDITION
1990

Typesetting by: Total Type & Graphics
        Berryville, AR 72616

Library of Congress Catalog Number: 90-63009
ISBN: 0-89221-188-1

DEDICATION

To my precious family
and to the Ladies Class at
Wisconsin Rapids Assembly for their
never-failing love and support.

PREFACE

This book is shared in hopes that those who read it will realize that the God we serve is not silent today. He is not unapproachable to us in our need; we do not wait in line for His attention or His blessing. He is there for us, each of us, in a wondrous, knowable, loving way, just waiting to be discovered, longing to be known and understood, desiring to share Himself and His deepest treasures with us, His children.

God loves us in our ordinariness; He delights in us and waits to speak to our deepest needs, even though we are only "us." We just need to learn to LISTEN. That is perhaps the difference between a child of God who "hears" God and one who does not. Do you know how to listen? Have you trained yourself to hear the still, small voice within you, or do you block it out with your busyness, with the noise and demands of the world, with your own apathy or unbelief?

I pray that the Lord will speak to hearts through the simple lessons He has shared with me. But my greatest hope and prayer is that these messages will serve to be stepping stones to your intimate sharing with the Lord, stepping stones to His intimate sharing with you. I pray that these pages will inspire a wholehearted search within you for the greatest treasure of all—knowing and communing with God Himself, for He waits to speak to you.

Pamela Steinke
1990

A BEGINNING

January 1   Lamentations 3:22-26

"There is a beginning to all things. Each goal must have its start in one simple first step. This is your first step—to meet alone with Me each and every day, no matter what the circumstances of that day. To block out the world entirely for that portion of time, to give Me lordship in your mind and heart, to give Me your undivided attention while I commune with you. All else will flow from that. If you honor Me with this obedient exercise every day your life will be changed! Your heart will be changed! Your goal will be realized."

CONSTANT COMMUNION

January 2   John 10:27; 16:12-15

"Do not think it strange that I speak to you so clearly. It is not strange nor should it be unusual. It is the way life was meant to be—in constant communion with Me. Only the world sees it as strange and impossible because they do not understand how I long to commune with them. They shut their ears and their hearts to Me by their unbelief, by their worldly viewpoint. Guard against this. Protect this precious gift between us by keeping your heart tender, by obeying Me in all things, by listening lovingly for My every whisper. I am meek and do not force Myself upon anyone."

I NEVER FAIL

January 3   1 Chronicles 28:20; Deuteronomy 31:8

"I will never fail you nor forsake you. If I turned My back on My children when they sinned, when they made wrong decisions, who would stand? Who would live through it? There is forgiveness in Me. There is hope! You must learn from your mistakes and failures though it be a hard lesson. You must learn to rely upon My wisdom, which is there for your protection. You must not turn from it again."

THE GREAT LIE

January 4   John 8:43-44; Psalm 34:8

"Do not let Satan tell you that I am boring! He tells this lie to the whole world. I am not boring! Only man's view of Me, his sometimes futile quest of Me, his idea of who and what I am, is boring. It is only when man stops at the threshold of really knowing Me, that he experiences boredom. Do not stay upon the threshold of experiencing Me—'taste and see that the Lord is good.' Don't let even one day slip by without experiencing Me. You do not know but that the experience of that very day could be the fragile link in the chain of events that I have planned so carefully for you. The words of that very day could form the fortress you need to face the next trial. My sharing that day could be the comfort you will need tomorrow."

THE ANSWER TO LIFE

January 5   John 14:6

"I am not just the answer to any single problem—I am the answer to life itself. You need Me every moment and I need you. How I love to reveal Myself to you, to lift the veil of the natural man from your eyes, to let you see Me, know Me, experience Me. Do not hold back—do not be afraid—it is good to be overwhelmed by My presence. It is a natural result of knowing Me. It is life-giving; it will bring health to your mind, body, and spirit. It will release you from all that binds you. Never doubt Me again. Have I not proven to you that I cannot fail you? Have I now earned your trust? Remember, that is all I ask of you—to trust Me and to obey Me. I will do the rest."

ONE HOUR

January 6   Matthew 6:6

"There is nothing so important in all of life that cannot be laid aside for just one hour each day. That is what I ask of you; to give one hour each day to your quest of Me. Lock yourself in with Me away from the demands of the world. This is a habit that must be formed. It was easy to do this when life was not so busy, but even more essential to do now.

"Hard, time-consuming work cannot be sustained for any length of time without periods of refreshment and rest, simple rest in Me. The refreshment of the Living Word, the loving Christ. Put this refreshment, this revitalizing intimacy with Me first before all else. Our sweet tender moments must not be sacrificed to anything else."

THE SEARCH

January 7   Jeremiah 29:13

"Search for Me with all your heart! That is the secret. A half-hearted search will never yield a harvest of knowing Me. Only those who seek with their whole heart, with everything in them concentrating upon Me, will ever really find Me. I must have first place in the hearts of My people. If they relegate any lesser place than that, that is also a degree of blessing, of knowledge of Me that they will receive. I can only work with what is given to Me. To the degree that a heart is opened up and yielded to Me, that is the degree to which I can fill and bless and work in that life. That is the degree to which they will hear My voice and enjoy My guidance."

THE ONLY MOLD

January 8   Psalm 149:4; 1 Corinthians 15:10

"It is okay to be **you**. It is okay to be you in the body of believers. I do not stamp believers out of one mold. No, each and every child of Mine is preciously different. It is all right to be who you are and where you are. That is what I delight in. Your relationship with Me is of utmost importance. Even your relationship with the church is secondary to that, as everything in life is secondary to our oneness. There are rough spots in your character, yes. There is rebellion in your heart, we both know that. But I am quite capable of handling those things in My own way. Do not worry about them. Just continue to love Me. I love you for yourself, for the unique personality that makes you, **you**! There are no molds in My kingdom—I have broken every one of them save one, My own image. And that image fits perfectly into each personality. Relax, and just let yourself love Me."

THE GREAT FRIEND

January 9   Psalm 139:17-18

"Come to Me with absolutely everything. That is what I am here for! No hurt is too small, no question too silly, no need too unimportant. Share every little event of life with Me. I listen to the details with perfect under-standing, unquestioning attention, undivided interest. All My time is yours—fill it with all of yourself, all of your life. I do not tire of you. Share all with Me, your Lord and Saviour, your confidante, the lover of your soul. Let us have many secrets, much shared joy, an abundance of love and laughter together."

COME UNTO ME

January 10   Ephesians 5:1

"I long to see the gentle stamp of My image upon the hearts of My people. I wait and long for this! Each shared moment, whether burden or victory, joy or sorrow, stamps the image ever deeper upon the life of My children. This is why I bid you come, come unto Me! Whether tired and weary, or filled with joy and wonder, or simply stepping along the path of life, come unto Me! I bring all things into balance. I fill every need. I chart every course. Let Me love you! Come unto Me!"

ESCAPE

January 11   Phillipians 2:5-8

"Escape? I do not call you to escape. That is not My way. Did I escape the challenges of My life? Did I escape the humble life, the human pain, the cross? No. And so, too, you must be willing to go through your life, not escape from it. I give refreshment along the way, I provide the temporary escapes necessary to refresh and restore you. But flight from the life I have chosen for you? No. You must face up to your life and walk in it, live through it, do what I have called you to do. There is no way out but My way—the path of simple obedience day by day."

MIND OF CHRIST

January 12   2 Corinthians 10:5

"You must control your thoughts. You must bring

every thought under My control. Is it a good thought, will it bless you? Will it bless others? Will it bring peace, joy, harmony, and success to life? If not, you have no business thinking it. Your thought-life must be pure, positive, activated by My Spirit, acceptable to the mind of Christ. It is not your place, as a child of God, to entertain negatives, to dwell on the bad things, to rob yourself of peace and power by thinking as Satan would have you think. Humble yourself then, by bringing every thought under My scrutiny, under My control. You will save yourself a lifetime of sorrow, of defeat, of failure."

THE GUARDED LIFE

January 13   Psalm 97:10; 125:2

"The guarded life, can you not feel it? Have you not known it all these years? You see My hand at every crossroad pointing the way. You feel My gentle touch at every resting place, My loving protection at every turn. The guarded life, My gift to you. My promise fulfilled, My love endowed, My longing satisfied. Yes, My child, I long for you to have the best of life, to be safe and happy and warm in My care! And so I am here, guarding, protecting, providing, loving, wrapping you up in the blanket of My love, sheltering you from the heat of the day, holding you through the watches of the night. Always ready to leap to your defense, always ready to guide and guard, always with you. This is My love, this is Me, this is the great **I AM**."

BLOCKED CHANNELS

January 14   1 John 1:9

"There must be nothing between us to stop the flow of

My Spirit to yours. Nothing blocking the flow of bless-ing—no disobedience, unconfessed sin, doubting or will-fulness. At all cost, keep this channel clear and free of rubbish! Then all blessing shall be yours, all that you need shall come to you unhindered. This is a physical law of My spiritual kingdom. Blocked channels prevent bless-ings and guidance from reaching you; they slow up progress and impede the pathway of your life. Make sure, that no matter what, there is nothing standing between My hand of blessing and your hand ready to receive. Remember, this is a law of the Kingdom, and you must learn to live by it. Then the greater secrets of the Kingdom shall be yours."

THE SHIP

January 15   Matthew 6:25-34

"Relax in Me. Do not struggle so! Live each moment as it comes, relaxing in the knowledge of My gentle care of you. There is no need to strain ahead, no need to vainly search the horizon for My next provision. It will come. As a ship sails into harbor, so shall My provision come. Rest easily in Me. Enjoy the blessings of the day, and leave the rest to Me. Could I ask a more simple thing of you? Yet, I know, the simple is often the most difficult. The simple task of faith and obedience requires the child-heart, the child-spirit, so rare within the heart of man, but so very necessary in My children."

TRUE FREEDOM

January 16   Phillippians 3:20-21

"Freedom from self—one of My most priceless gifts! This is My gift to you this day. Freedom to rise above this life, this temporary home of earth. Freedom to enjoy My presence, My home, in your spirit. Freedom from fear, from worry, from all that binds My people to this world. That is the freedom I offer to you.

"Walk the high places with Me, your Lord. Step lightly upon earth's crust, knowing that truly you walk the heavenlies with Me."

THE BALANCED LIFE

January 17   Proverbs 4:27

"Equilibrium. That is the essence of My message for your life. Balance in all things—balance of the heart and mind and passions. To be set out boldly in the winds of life and circumstance and neither bend nor falter. To remain solid and upright, at peace, no matter how the winds blow, no matter what dark cloud threatens in the distance. Just to stand and stay standing. Plant your feet solidly upon the Rock. Let the winds blow about you with all their force. They have no power to harm you, for I am your rock. I am your anchor. Let Me be your peace, your power, your stabilizer. Bend neither to the right nor to the left, but receive your balance in Me."

ONE DAY AT A TIME

January 18   Proverbs 27:1

"Why so impatient? Can you not live one day at a time with Me? Do you think life is to be worked out, lived through and conquered all in one day? Even My life could not be lived thus. No, true life must be lived one moment at a time. There is no other way. There are no shortcuts, no easy answers, no magic carpet ride to bypass daily living."

UMPIRE

January 19   Colossians 3:15; Philippians 4:8

"Yes! Stay in control of your thoughts! That is the secret to peace and happiness. If your thoughts are in control of you, then there is trouble. You are the master of your own mind. Nothing can enter in that you do not allow. Continue to let Me be the umpire in your heart and mind."

BRING THE NEED

January 20   Isaiah 58:11; 1 Peter 2:24

"Come to Me for all that you need. Come to Me to be renewed! Do you lack strength? Come to Me for more. Is your peace ebbing away through the cracks of disappointment and trial? Come to Me for even greater peace. Are you losing confidence? I am here to lift you up. Is it love that you lack, or joy or patience or trust or guidance? It matters not what the need may be—I fill them all. Bring the need that I may fill it.

"That is why this time together is so vital. It is the time of renewal, of refilling, of receiving. It is a time of blessing! A time for you to be restored to peace and balance, no matter what support the world has kicked out from under you. No matter how deeply you have been hurt or disappointed, I can fill in that emptiness. I can heal the wound, no matter how deep. Always I work to bring you back to that place of perfect balance and peace where you deserve to live."

UNHAPPINESS

January 21   Philippians 4:11

"You must realize that no circumstances in life have

the power to make you unhappy. It is only your attitude toward the circumstance, your failure to trust Me in that circumstance, that causes unhappiness. Things or situations in themselves have no power over you. You are the one who chooses where the power lies—whether it be in self, in circumstances, or in Me. Where will you have that power lie?"

DULL DAYS

January 22   Romans 5:1-2

"Yes, I speak to you on the dull days as well as on the glorious ones! It matters not to Me. As long as your heart is open to receive My message, I am here. I wait to speak peace and comfort, love and counsel. I bring all the powers and wonders of heaven with Me. They are at your disposal. Wherever I am, there also is My power, My light, My strength, My love. Think of the benefit of calling those things into action—just by being with Me. Just by spending time in My presence, by allowing Me to fill you, to befriend you, to be yours."

RESPONSIBILITY

January 23   Ephesians 1:4-5

"It is My responsibility to care for you; did you think I was just being kind? Kind, yes, but more than that! You are My charge, My adopted child—it is My responsibility and My delight to take care of you. You have given Me everything, every part of yourself. Could I do any less for you? You think I owe you nothing, but My love does owe you; it owes you all that I possess. Take freely of My treasure!"

WISDOM

January 24   James 1:5

"I share My wisdom with you gladly, abundantly! Come to Me for continual wisdom!"

THE LITTLE FAITH

January 25   Mark 9:24

"Arise. Awaken the little faith within you and walk with Me. I will hold your hand a little tighter, I will slow My steps a bit to match yours, I will make up for the lack of faith within you. I will put My own faith, My own love, My own strength, in its place until you are filled to overflowing. I love you unconditionally. My love and understanding are not based upon the strength of your faith. They are based solely upon the depth of My love. Do not be ashamed. Confess your doubts and come forward from the tomb of self-pity to walk in the sunlight with Me. Come on; come out of there and take My hand once more and we will be on our way. Everything is all right. You will see. Everything will be all right."

ALL-ENCOMPASSING LOVE

January 26   Romans 8:35-39

"Do I take My love from you for even an instant? No! That is a lie of Satan. My love is firm, constant, all-encompassing. It does not depend upon your feelings or your performance. It depends only upon Me, and I am unchanging. I have given My love to you and there it shall stay, no matter what. It is yours. No one can steal it from you, not even Satan himself. You cannot lose it or give it back. My love surrounds you like an ocean, fills you like a river, sticks to you like glue! Rest in My love, accept My forgiveness, accept My discipline. All is well."

THE PLANNED LIFE

January 27   Psalm 25:12; 31:14-16

"Everything is of My planning in your life. Each day, each person you meet, each trial, each joy. All brought together through one great network of caring for you. All sifted through My love, My plan for you. There is no chance happening, no unimportant event, no uselessness in a life directed by Me.

"Go through each day, then, confident of My planning, My guidance, and My protection. Yours is a planned life, a blessed life, a life held lovingly in My hand."

FOLLOW

January 28   Romans 8:14

"Inch by inch, follow closely, carefully, each instruction, each little urging of My Spirit. If you are not sure of the Spirit's voice, stop whatever you are doing and ask Me. More and more you will know for sure the voice of the Spirit and that of self. It is a delicate lesson but so essential to your walk with Me. And so important to follow each urging of My Spirit. It will save you great heartache. It will ensure you of great success."

THE ORDERED LIFE

January 29   Romans 8:28

"The ordered life. Are there any chance happenings,

any `luck,' in the lives of My children? I think not! The ordered life—planned by Me, guided by My Spirit—this is your privilege. I love to plan for you. This is My privilege, My joy!"

THE TANTRUM

January 30   Psalm 107:13-22

"I want to reveal to you why you are having such a difficult time having faith in this situation. It is because you are not accepting the circumstances of your life as they are.

"You are not accepting the fact that this is the way that I want your life right now. I have My reasons. Yes, I have promised to help you, but it will be in My way and in My timing. Until then, you must learn to put a smile on your face, stop stamping that foot at Me, and stop whining and crying. You are meeting your problems like a sissy. Focus your attention on Me, on the beautiful world I have given you, on the lovely family you have, on your work, on all the precious good things in life. Let yourself feel My strength and peace. You scurry into your corner of fear and doubt and despair, and there is no comfort there. Can you not learn this?"

THE ULTIMATE REQUIREMENT

January 31   Proverbs 3:5-6

"The final test, the ultimate victory, the beginning, the middle, the end—that is trust. Trust is everything in the lives of My children. It is both the basic and the ultimate requirement. Without it, life is sad, confusing defeat. With it, life is one golden moment after another. Moments of excitement, peace, joy, the thrill of seeing the hand of God at work. The peace of knowing that I am in control."

THE CALMNESS OF CHRIST

February 1   Romans 8:6

"All must be calm—the heart, the mind, the spirit. So is the person who lives his life in Me. Calm that I might speak in the quietness, calm that I might do My work unhampered. It is much to ask, I know. But more and more this calmness of Christ must be a part of your life. So much more will be accomplished in this way, My way. I am in control. You must know this, you must believe it in order to have My serenity in your life."

ALL IS WELL

February 2   Proverbs 3:25

"All is well! Say it often, in the midst of heartache, chaos and fear. All is well. Know that no matter what the circumstance, because I am with you all is well. Look at this world through the eyes of Christ. See with your spiritual vision. Know in your heart that nothing is out of My control, nothing is beyond My intervention. You are safe in Me."

THE FOG

February 3   Proverbs 4:18

"Only My people who are not trained to listen to Me, operate in a fog. The fog will lift as you go along in quiet trust, step by step with the Master."

REST

February 4   Matthew 11:28

"Rest for the soul, rest for the weary. That is My

provision. Rest in the midst of trouble, heartache, confusion, work. Rest in the midst of any and every circumstance of life. That is My great gift to a weary world, but is so often neglected and unclaimed by even My closest friends. They think this rest must be worked for, when truly it need only be accepted—just like salvation. The rest is here in Me. By sharing My life you share My rest. But is it any wonder that so few share this rest? So few really take the time and effort to be with Me. That is the secret. This rest comes only through contact with Me. It cannot be magically dropped upon you, or poured over you. It is only the natural result of sharing time with Me. There is no other instant way to receive it! Do you see then why I said, `Come unto Me?' It is the only way that man can receive the rest I have promised."

DOUBT

February 5   John 8:43-44

"When you doubt Me, you are believing Satan. You do not just doubt Me, but you believe him! You either believe Me or you believe the `father of lies.' There is no middle road. Whom do you choose to believe? Does not My Word say that there is no truth in him? Do not be deceived."

NO CONDEMNATION

February 6   Romans 8:1

"You are letting feelings of guilt stand between us. Yes, you have made mistakes and rash decisions, but you have seen your mistakes and I have forgiven you. Do not sorrow over it anymore. You have made the mistake, but I will work it out for I cannot fail you. Stop condemning yourself and trust Me. You must accept My complete forgiveness as Peter did after his denial of Me.

"I always meet My children where they are at. We must go on from here, for you must never let the realization of sin in your life come between us. I saw the sin long before you did, and paid for it long ago. The important thing is to look at Me so closely from now on, that the sin is not repeated."

CAST OUT FEAR

February 7   1 John 4:18

"Every step of faith can produce fear. Every change seeks to unsettle My children. But rise above fear; break free of it!

" `Perfect love casts out all fear.' Come to Me as with all else and let Me cast it out. Let Me be your refuge, your strong fortress to which you can run. Trust Me! Be a `fool' for My sake—in the end you will see. I am excited for you to see."

JUDGE NOT

February 8   Romans 14:10; 14:13

"Remember, you must follow Me. Each life is different. Do not envy those whose lives seem easier or more blessed, and in the same way, do not feel guilty or fearful when you see someone whose life is filled with difficulty or tragedy. Do not judge your life and your circumstances by the blessings or trials in another's life. These things must be left up to Me. It is not for you to judge or figure out—you are only to follow Me in your life each moment."

CHAIN OF THE KINGDOM

February 9   Matthew 26:39

"Do not rebel or attempt to escape the life I have chosen for you. Submit to Me, to My choices for you. I have told you that each person in your life is placed there by Me. Fit in with My plans, accept My blessings and also what I give you to bear. No one else in this world can fill your link in My chain of the kingdom. Accept your place, therefore; fulfill your mission by simply loving and letting Me do the rest. Accept, love, follow, rest!"

POUR YOURSELF OUT

February 10   Colossians 3:23-24

"Pour yourself out into all that I give you to do. In doing so there is great reward. Pour yourself out!"

THE ONE GREAT GOAL

February 11   1 John 2:15

"More and more I become your all. More and more the threads of our lives are woven together in beautiful, intricate patterns of love! More and more we grow closer, in heart and soul and spirit. Everything in life is leading us to this one great goal—absolute oneness. My heart sings to see it! There is no greater joy, no greater fulfillment, no greater wonder, than to be one with Me. And there is no greater pleasure than to be one with you. My goal, My desire, My pleasure, is wrapped up in you, in the lives of My dear ones. Care not for the things of this world. They are but a by-product of life—I am the true life."

EACH ONE

"I died for you that day on the Cross. I did not die for a mass of people I could not distinguish. No, I died for you individually, as I speak to you individually now. And so it is with all My children. I died for each of them, not all of them. There is a difference. And I live for each of them now. That is why I can know and love and speak to each heart alone! Will heaven be any different, you have wondered? Would I trade this oneness, this individual relationship, for a group relationship? Never! No, our oneness here leads only to greater oneness there. Nothing will be lost, but everything will be gained. You will know Me! You will see Me! Our personal, individual relationship will continue, not be swallowed up by the masses. I am able to do this. I would have it no other way!"

THE CHOICE

"It is your choice. You may choose to look at your life through the eyes of those around you, or you may choose to see through My eyes. You have the right to choose, it is true. But choose wisely.

"How do you feel after looking at things through earthly eyes? Does it make you happy? Or do you suddenly find yourself in the pit of discouragement and self-pity?

"I have so much more for you. My way of seeing things is so freeing, so blessed. Please use the vision of faith, of love, of joyful trust in Me. Do not yield to temptation—be strong in your trust, in your spiritual vision. See things through My eyes. Let your life rest in Me and I will take care of you far better than you could ever take care of yourself, far better than anyone in this world could take care of you. Leave the choices and all the details to Me. Go forward into life, blissfully unafraid. Let the world choose its own course—you have chosen to follow Me."

THE SOURCE

February 14   Matthew 16:26

"You must learn where your happiness lies. True lasting happiness does not lie in circumstance. It is not found in money or possessions or in time spent on one-self. The only pure and eternal happiness resides in Me. Do not look upon the things of this world as your source of joy, and then you will never be disappointed. A certain measure of joy does come from these earthly pursuits, but let that be just a bonus, an addition to My true joy!"

THE LIFELINE

February 15   John 14:6; Psalm 37:3

"I am the lifeline to link you up with true life—the peace and joy and blessed calmness of life with Me. Hang onto the lifeline—do not let it slip from your grasp. Do not let it be pulled from your hands when you are not watch-ing. Hang onto the lifeline! We will skim the dark waters but never go under. You are safe, guided, protected in My care."

CIRCUMSTANCE

February 16   Galatians 5:1

"Circumstance. Just a word, simply stated. Not an iron chain binding you to earth. Circumstance is the stuff life is made of, but not life itself. Real life is so far above circumstance, that circumstance has no power over it. Accept the circumstances of your life then, but do not fear them. Do not let them bind you to earth. Release yourself to Me—I am true freedom. I am power—I am life. Be free in Me."

PLANNING

February 17   Proverbs 3:5; Psalm 25:12

"My ways are not your ways. My knowledge is all-encompassing, my wisdom and foresight unmatched; My planning and guidance unequaled. Do not depend upon your own wisdom and planning. Depend only upon Me."

IMPATIENCE

February 18   Psalm 40:1

"I understand impatience. I know that it is difficult to wait. But life is made up of waiting. That is a part of trust and growth. The lesson that must be learned is to enjoy life and live it to its fullest each moment—as you wait. I take you through life just one step at a time, no more. Will I not work out the results of what I have begun to do in your life? Do I expect you to jump ahead of Me and do more than I ask of you each day? No! To do so is to depend upon yourself and your own judgment, instead of on Me. The way of the Kingdom is often a slow way. As I always tell you, just trust Me."

FILTHY RAGS

February 19   Colossians 3:8; Ephesians 4:26

"As long as you hold one shred of anger against

another, you are not trusting Me fully. You must realize this for your own good. Any anger, blame, judging against another, is not faith in Me. You must let go of all of it. I want it all so that I can cast it into the sea. How you feel compelled to cling to these things! That is a part of human nature, but as you give me your nature, I give you My God nature. Trade all that holds you back for all that will change your life. Trade all the miseries you hang onto for all the choice blessings of My kingdom. And what a trade it is! Filthy, torn rags for exquisite pearls! These are the only trades I offer My children—their worst for My best. Has mankind ever see such a bargain?"

PROPER ORDER

February 20   Psalm 127:1-2

"Give the control of your time and your life to Me, not to the world. It is true that I have given you much to do, but these things must be done in proper order. They must not gain control over you or your life.

"Trust Me, I will help you. Let Me be the Master of your schedule, the Great Organizer and Teacher and Friend. Just hang onto Me and let Me go first. Let Me arrange and prepare the way for you as you cling to My robes. You are on a great and challenging path which I have prepared for you. Let Me go before you for I already know the way before you come to it! Enjoy the peace of knowing that you are in the place I have chosen for you. Continue to follow Me; that is all I ask."

DETAILS

February 21   Ecclesiastes 7:14; Proverbs 27:1

"Live each day as it comes, for Me and with Me. Do not worry about tomorrow or about any day in the future.

Live only in today, doing those things each day that you know I want you to do. Then just trust Me; I will work everything out and will take care of all the details. Leave the details to Me."

THE PROVIDER

February 22   Psalm 34:9-10; Matthew 6:25-26

"Your concern must be to be the person I want you to be, the mate, the parent, the friend, that I call you to be. You must not concern yourself with these other things— I will take care of them! I am your Provider. I am the provider you yearn for. Do not concern yourself about these things—this is My command to you!

"I have said that I am your Provider, and I make no shallow claims. But I have also said that your faith unlocks My provision. You must not whine and struggle as you wait for the need to be met; just rest quietly in Me. Remember, obedience and faith are the keys which release My supply. Honor Me with your trust, for this is obedience in action. Keep obeying, keep trusting, keep believing."

STRETCHING

February 23   Proverbs 3:5-6; 4:25-26

"Go along in quiet trust, doing those things necessary to life each day. Then I will show you all that you need to know. The way will be made clear; the means will be provided, the guidance will be given at the proper time. This is the way that all of life should be lived, one step at a time, one step behind Me, holding My hand as you follow. That is all I ask of you. It hurts not to know the future all at once, I know. It stretches you, it stretches your faith. And in the midst of all the stretching, growth becomes character, and character becomes godliness, and that is our goal."

GODLY RESTRAINT

February 24   Psalm 3:8

"I cannot whisk all your problems away instantly with a touch of glory. When I say `cannot,' I do not mean that I lack the power to do that. But for your good and because of the restraint I must sometimes use in earthly matters, I do not always find it best to do so. But remember, I do not change, and I have promised to be your provider. Just keep going along the path I have charted for you. Go on in faith and trust. The world is powerless to hurt you, for I am your protector. I give the strength necessary to meet the demands of the need you face. Keep relying upon Me, keep hoping in Me. As I have said before, `You shall see my deliverance.'"

NOURISHMENT

February 25   Psalm 1:3

"Do you see now how everything I allow to come into your life is for your good? Even the disappointments, the failures, the seemingly unanswered prayers, are for your greater benefit! The tree of blessing must get its nourishment from the roots deep below the surface where no sun can shine. Even so, sometimes your greatest nourishment must come from the seeming disappointments and difficulties of life. Let your roots run deep down into Me so that I may channel all these dark moments of life into sweet spiritual nourishment and provision."

THE GOOD SHEPHERD

February 26   John 10:11; 10:28-29

"Always I carry you in the palm of My hand. **Always** I carry you! I do not let go of you—I do not set you down to see how you fare on your own. No, this is not My way. Those who teach such things are mistaken; they do not understand the Good Shepherd. You have nothing to prove on your own, for only in the palm of My hand can you meet and conquer the difficulties of life. I do not send you off to conquer on your own, while I watch from a distance. Such treatment would be foolish and cruel. I not only go with you, but I carry you through the difficulties, through the winding path of life. I cherish you!"

BE COMPLETE

February 27   Psalm 62:1-2

"Give Me all your concerns. Then do not pick them up again. When you give them to Me, I take them. I do not walk away from your outstretched hand. I take what is in it! I take it for My own and I deal with it. I use miraculous means if I must, but I do deal with it in the best possible way. How foolish for you to take it back again even for a moment. Leave all this with Me. I am your salvation. I am your love, I am your life—I am all to you. Rejoice in My love! Rest in My greatness which is displayed on your behalf. Be complete in Me, for I am your completion. I am all that you seek, all that you hunger and thirst for, all that your spirit cries out to have, all that your soul yearns to possess. **I AM**."

THE MOUNTAINTOP OF FAITH

February 28   Psalm 90:1; 91:1

"You have risen out of the valley of despair to the

mountaintop of faith in Me. Up here you can see beyond the valley, past the problems and the fears and doubts of despondency. This is your rightful home, your dwelling place in Me. I have bought it for you, and the purchase price was My own blood. You may stay here with Me for the rest of your life, for it is My gift to you. Do not go back to the valley, for you do not belong there anymore. Why do you insist upon living there in the dark valley of despair, when this mountaintop home in the sunshine is yours?

"It is your choice. I will not force you to stay. You must choose whether to turn away and journey back to the valley, or to stay here in this lovely home that your faith provides for you. Stay with Me, for up here you will see the valley through My eyes, as we face it together."

SHARING

March 1   1 Peter 1:8-9; 1:22

"Share your life, your love, with others. Share what you know of Me. The explanation of how you know, of what I say to you, is not always necessary. What is necessary is that these lessons produce a life in you that reflects Me. A life yielded to and guided by Me will draw others to Me. Your actions will mean much more than your words ever could. These times shared with Me in sweet communion will produce a joy welling up inside you—a joy that will burst forth no matter what the circumstance, and that will speak for itself."

THE STORYBOOK LIFE

March 2   1 Peter 4:1-2

"I choose the roles a person is to have in life. It is not always according to the book, nor does it always follow the fantasy existence that people believe in as children.

You must accept this hard fact of life if you are to be joyful. The storybook life is for heaven, not for the school of life here on earth. Each person has fairy tales that he must give up in order to face and deal with the reality of his own existence. Dare to dream, but not at the expense of your happiness in the present."

THE HEALER

March 3   Matthew 9:12

"I am the One who reshapes twisted lives, who puts the pieces back together according to the master plan. I am your teacher, your healer, your physician. I want to heal, to make your life whole and happy. That is part of My plan. When My children lay heavy burdens upon themselves, I am forced to sit and wait for them to seek Me. I cannot force them to use My wisdom, but when they later come to Me in tears, with the threads of their lives and dreams twisted in hopeless knots, do you think I turn My back on them? Do you think I leave them to figure out the knotted strands by themselves when they ask for My help? When one repents and seeks to trust Me, do you think I turn from them as they had turned from Me? No! I am not a man. I am a God of endless love and compassion. Every day is a new beginning in My kingdom."

TATTERED SHREDS

March 4   Psalm 55:22

"Bring Me the tattered shreds of your life, the twisted threads of your existence, the hopelessly inadequate supply of strength you have left! Give it all to Me in one great heap and pick it up no more. Empty your hands of this burden once and for all, so that I can fill them with all good things to enjoy. Trade in the burden, the guilt, the inadequacies, for My peace, My joy, My supply. You cannot carry both the burdens and the supply at the same time, for man is capable of carrying just one thing at a time. Let go and receive."

POWERFUL PRAISE

March 5   Psalm 22:3

"When the world seems to be tumbling down around your feet, praise Me! Reach out with arms of faith, throw caution to the wind, and burst out in praises to your Saviour. Praises defeat the power of the enemy, for I inhabit the praises of My people. Can Satan dwell with God? Therefore, let your praises resound, let the joyful noise of praise ring out across your world, and your world shall be conquered. In the name of Jesus it shall be so! There is great power, great release in praising Me. My power, when called upon in praise, bursts forth to aid and comfort, to help and work. My power is released by the praises of My people."

THE PACK

March 6   1 Peter 5:7; Psalm 55:22

"Leave your burdens in My pack. I have them safely gathered up inside and I will carry them for you. You were wise to let me hold them for you—be wiser still and let Me **keep** them. I will carry them; I will look in on them to see how they are doing; I will work out their solutions and take them out of My bag as they are solved. Don't worry, I will keep track of them for you. Don't give it a thought. I will take care of everything!"

ASK

"Pray for things! Ask Me for what you need, believing that you will receive it. To trust without asking is laziness. I will meet all your needs, but I require you to ask, to knock, to seek.

"Think of the joy you experience when you ask specifically and I answer specifically. This gives life with Me its spice, its charm, its wonder.

"Do not doubt that I will answer. My answer may not always be exactly what you expected, but I will answer. The closer you get to Me, the more answers you will receive, for you are then so in tune with Me that you know and pray according to My will."

USE ME

"I do not mind being `used.' It is My greatest joy, for My life was given to be used, not just to be talked about. Use Me then without feeling guilty, without feeling unworthy, without any hesitation. That is what I want. I never tire of your requests—I wait for them. I never get sick of hearing the same problems over and over—I am here to listen."

THE UNCLUTTERED HEART

"As I said to Martha, I say to you—don't worry so about all the little details of life. Leave those things to Me. Lay them aside, sit at My feet in your spirit and learn from Me. That is the important part of life. Then the doing of

My will, the obedient, happy trust will follow as a result of you following Me.

"I know and care more about the details of your life than you will ever know. I am always there before you, working things out."

BE CONSUMED

March 10   Isaiah 26:3

"Yes, be consumed, but not by fears, not by worries, not by frustration. Be consumed by My love, My peace, My joy so unlike that of the world. Be consumed by My Spirit filling you totally, and activating all you think and say and do. Be consumed by the positives of life, by the riches of My grace, by your love for Me and My love for you."

THIS DAY

March 11   Psalm 92:4-5

"Enjoy each day as it comes! Those who live in the future waste so much of real life. They exist on daydreams and future plans and longing for things to come, while life slips silently by unnoticed, and their todays are swallowed up by their tomorrows. For only the `tomorrows' seem appealing to them.

"It is today that must be given your all. You do well to slow down and open up your senses to the wonder of **this** day. You have been learning this with the wonder of a child, and My heart sings for you! I give the pleasures of sunshine and flowers and warmth and water and growing things, to bless you, to make you happy, to erase some of the heartache of living in a fallen world. I delight in seeing My children enjoy My gifts to them."

THE POSITIVES

March 12   Philippians 4:8; Ephesians 6:10-11

"Yes, dwell much upon the positives! Let the good things of life saturate your mind; think much about them and do not give thought to the negative. Always think upon the positive. Concentrate upon each blessing until you are filled with joy! Always you have concentrated most upon the negatives of life. Now it is time to learn to fill your thoughts with the good. You are learning to wear the armor of God."

BE STILL

March 13   Psalm 37:7

"Just be still before Me. Put Me first in your heart and be still. Empty yourself of all other thoughts but Me, as I emptied Myself for you when I became man. Rest in My presence so that I can fill you. I cannot fill a heart that is already full, full of the things of the world. I can only fill empty, waiting vessels. Do not let the world crowd Me out of My rightful place."

EACH DAY

March 14   2 Corinthians 11:3

"You must do each day what I give you to do. Then you cannot go wrong. Just follow Me—that is all. It is as easy as that—the simplicity of Christ! Only I know the working of My plan, the glad surprises along the way. And only I can share them with you as you leave your mind and heart open to Me, to My will. Follow the urging of My Spirit in regard to this. Remember, follow Me each day. You cannot follow for days and months and years all at once, but only each day as I give it to you. That is the secret happiness of a full life in My service."

THE FATHER OF LIES

March 15   John 8:43-44

"Does this feeling of uneasiness spring from Me? Do I wish for you to be uneasy, doubtful, nervous? No! These feelings, these temptations, spring directly from the father of lies, and from your own insecurity. Your security must lie in Me, in My promises to you. Have we not been over this many times before? You must cast out these anxious feelings, destroy these troubling thoughts before they reach full fruition. Do not permit them to take root, or you will once again need deliverance from their oppression! Do not let them take root. Cast aside the darts of Satan—get behind the shield I provide. Do not let him get a foothold for he is as a prowling lion about you. Keep him on the outside of the camp. Let him growl and threaten—he does no harm there. It is only when he is allowed entrance that he steals, kills and destroys."

THE ANSWER

March 16   Phillipians 4:11; 1 Timothy 6:8

"You must find your satisfaction in Me. You must settle down in your spirit, give every part of yourself and your life totally to My care and keeping, and accept life as I give it to you. There is no other way to true contentment. There will be no contentment until you do this.

"Are you uneasy about what must be done in your business? Come to Me for direction. Are there difficulties with finances? Come to Me for My provision. Are you bored, restless, uncertain? Come to Me no matter what the problem. There are no answers but those found in Me.

Is there a need I cannot fill? No, I tell you, there is not!"

NEW BEGINNINGS

March 17   Hebrews 8:12; 10:19-23

"It is a beginning—a new beginning, as each day can be. This is My gift to you—new beginnings as often as you have need of them. I do not begrudge you; take as many as you need along the way. Begin again this very day. I say this with joy, with love, even with laughter! I am so glad to have you back where you belong. Do not let Satan hang clouds of guilt or doubt upon your heart. The is **our** day, a day of rejoicing! Let us go on from here. Let us leave Satan behind in the dust where he belongs. Take My hand, lift up your head, look into My eyes—see the love, the joy, the forgiveness there? Then come, follow Me! Come, take My hand and follow Me."

NEED OF THE MOMENT

March 18   Hebrews 4:16; Matthew 6:27

"The need of the moment. That is what I provide for. One moment at a time. There is no need until we get there. Anticipating a future need is not a present need. The present need is for peace and rest while I take care of the future need."

THE MEASURE

March 19   John 14:15, 21

"Simple obedience. That is the measure of all things—have you obeyed? Obedience is not usually glamorous, it is not always exciting and it is rarely easy. But it is what

I require of you. Obedience in the little things. In simple ways, in all that you do. To live each moment as I have taught you, no matter what the circumstance. This must be the goal—the simplicity of Christ. The simplicity of obedience."

THE NECESSITY OF NEED

March 20   Philippians 4:19

"Where would you be without the need in your life? Would you be at My feet, learning of the Saviour, or would I find you elsewhere, pursuing your own narrow interests? There are many needs in the life of man—physical, mental, emotional, spiritual—all of them met by Me. All of them meant to bring you closer to the One who loves you most."

TAKE TIME

March 21   Psalm 32:6; 19:14

"Take time. All time is from Me. Take, therefore, the time I give so liberally, and share it with Me! Give Me the first part of your time. I promise peace, joy, counsel and great blessing if you obey Me in this."

UNCONDITIONAL LOVE

March 22   1 John 4:8

"I am love. Love has no limits, no boundaries, no conditions placed upon it. It is there, rich and free, for those who possess Me. There is no change in My love, no vacillation, no end. This is the love that follows you all the days of your life, the love that engulfs you, that satisfies all the needs and desires of your heart."

WAVES

March 23   Matthew 13:58

"Do not look upon the waves. That is Satan's territory. Look only to Me. Live in constant expectation of My miracles. Then miracles you shall have."

GUIDANCE

March 24   Mark 1:12

"There is no easy way to My guidance. Guidance means time spent with Me, a heart turned to Me, a life lived in Me. Then the guidance is absorbed into your heart and will as you abide. That is the only way. That is My way. That is the way that even I received guidance from My Father. Should it then be any different for you?"

MATCHLESS TREASURES

March 25   Psalm 104:28; Matthew 6:8

"My heart thrills at the thought of helping you! It is one of My greatest pleasures as Creator and Lord. Creating solutions to your problems and satisfying you with all good things.

"The beauty, the joy, that you sense all around you today is but a brief glimpse into the heart of God! There are matchless treasures deep within My heart that are just waiting to be discovered by My children. Just take the time to look, to explore, to watch and wait quietly in My presence, and suddenly it is revealed to you. Suddenly you know more of Me, the priceless treasure you seek."

THE MIGHTY SHIELD

March 26   Psalm 3:3; 5:3

"Yes, My child, this is the great love relationship I seek to have with My children. To curl up beside you each morning, to hold you close to Me and prepare and strengthen you for the new day. Thank you for your kind invitation! It is My privilege to draw up close to you, to ride the long miles with you, to walk beside you each step of life's way.

"It is an honor to share your life—an honor that few people extend to Me. I cherish our moments together. I live for them. I died for them! Never let an ounce of doubt pass between us. My love is a mighty shield."

NEGATIVES

March 27   Romans 8:5

"Cast all negatives from your vicinity before they take up residence in your mind! Do not allow them to even wipe their feet on your welcome mat, much less open the door to them. Banish them from the kingdom of your heart—My kingdom."

BECOMING ONE

March 28   John 14:20-21; Matthew 6:7-8

"More and more we are becoming one. Can you not feel it as we go through our days together? That warmth, that closeness, the understanding shared, the quiet trust that you place in Me as obstacles arise. More and more you look to Me for the answers, for wisdom, for direction.

"Just rest awhile in the warm gentle glow of our love. This resting in Me, this soaking up of My presence, will mean more to you than many hours of feverish petition. There is no need for feverish petition when a heart is so close to Mine. The mere whisper of My name, `Jesus,' and I rush to your aid with the solution that was planned before the need was even recognized by you!"

GOD OF HOPE

March 29   Psalm 33:20-22; 1 Peter 2:24

"My cross is large enough to cover all your sins, past, present, and forever. I know that you get disappointed in yourself—this is the mark of a tender conscience. Be thankful for this. Come before Me for forgiveness and cleansing and let Me wash away not only the sin, but the disappointment also. I am a God of hope. Place your hope for future holiness in Me, not in your own feeble attempts at holiness."

OPEN DOORS

March 30   Jeremiah 29:11

"Are you beginning to realize that your love for Me opens many doors? Doors of blessing and answered prayer, doors to provision and success. How can I turn down a heart of love? A heart filled with precious bubbling love for Me? I cannot! Oh, that does not always mean that every request will be granted in just the way you would want. Those who are mature in faith know that this is not possible or best for them. Because of My great love, I must make the final decision, for I know best. I know the future and I know My plan, and those who love Me the most are secure in My choices for them. This is becoming more and more your way of life and prayer— seeking My choices, My will. I thank you for this. How it frees Me to be able to do My best for you."

ANY LOVE

March 31   Galatians 5:22

"Any form of love you wish to give Me is gladly accepted! Never be afraid that it is too unworthy or too meager. Any love, no matter how minute, becomes as precious as pure gold as it leaves your heart to meet Mine."

THE SHARED LIFE

April 1   John 17:26

"Oh yes! It gives Me such great joy to work all things out for you. To see a faint glimmer of faith and hope blossom into full grown trust in Me. To know the rejoicing in your heart, to share the excitement of answered prayer with you. How I love you! How I long to please you as you are longing to please Me. This is the great relationship I seek to have with My children. Let us please each other; let us share our lives; let us be one as the Father and I are one."

TREASURES

April 2   Psalm 127:2; Luke 13:34

"Above all, continue to love Me! Your soul and spirit cry out to Me in the half-sleep of a new day. The first thoughts to fill your mind each morning are thoughts of Me. Your tender turning to Me throughout the day, your longing to serve and satisfy My every desire for you—these are the treasures My heart holds. I will care for you as a mother nurses her tender newborn. I will satisfy your heart's desire, your spirit's restlessness. As you turn to Me in love and gentle trust, I will be your all. I cannot fail you—I will not fail a heart of love, a heart that loves Me for Myself."

PRECIOUS TIME

April 3   Exodus 20:5; Psalm 5:3

"Do you think I try to steal your time from you? No! I make your time more precious, far more valuable than it could ever be otherwise. You must share your time with Me so that I can share Myself with you. Tithe your time to Me each day. This is far more valuable than any other tithe could be. Set the first part of each day aside for Me before the world and the care of life crowd in and crowd Me out. Then you will be able to go through the day with My blessing, doing all that must be done with no guilty thoughts hanging over you because of your selfishness. Do not hoard your time, for it must be My time also. I paid for it with My very life, and I am jealous over it. Give Me what is Mine, and I will give you all that I have in return."

FREE OF FEAR

April 4   Psalm 116:15; 1 Corinthians 15:54

"Think about this. Why does death hold no fear for you? Because you are trusting Me to care for you when it comes, right? Are you rushing around making preparations for your death? No! You are leaving all that to Me. Do you see? Life is to be the same way! My Word says that I am Lord of both life and death. In the same way that you trust Me with your death, so trust Me with your life! Am I not capable of both? Do you see it now?

"As you do not live in fear of death, so do not live in fear of life. There is nothing to fear in Me. You are learning—keep trusting."

THE BEAUTIFUL LIFE

April 5   Isaiah 51:11

"Make all of life, all that you do, a thing of beauty. A treasure held in the hands of God. This can be done through simple, joyful, obedience and trust in Me. The simplest task, the lowliest assignment, the most routine day, becomes a golden opportunity, a treasured time of communion with Me—just by a change in attitude, just by going through the day with My joy in your heart. All of life becomes a treasure when faced with My joy, My endless, boundless joy. Make it more a part of you, of your way of seeing things.

"Life is not meant to be a loathsome burden; it is meant to be a joyful stepping up to greater joy, eternal joy, in My presence. This life is merely a stepping stone to greater life, to eternal life, the ultimate calling."

THE INNER CORE

April 6   Ephesians 5:18

"Stay involved with Me. Do not ever be a part of the `fringe' that stays on the sidelines of experience with Me. Be in the inner core of My kingdom. Be saturated with Me, with My Spirit, and My ways. Be filled with My presence, be overwhelmed with My love, be ever listening and responsive to My every whisper. Let yourself be wrapped up in Me. Then so many opportunities will present themselves. You have already seen for a long time how I am always planning for you, always working things out in your life, even to the smallest detail and timing. Enjoy this caring, this planning that I do for you as I enjoy it. It is a precious service to Me, to care and plan for you. The intricacies of the working out of My plan in your life are exciting to Me—just live and love and let Me do My work."

NO VAIN SEARCH

April 7   Jeremiah 29:11

"Seek Me daily. Then all else will come.The wisdom, knowledge, and guidance necessary to your calling. It shall all be made evident as you come to Me. You are not meant to be on a vain search. There is no reason for that. I know the way so follow Me. Yes, a pity that we may only go one day at a time, but that is the way of this world. Much is learned by this daily process, this moment by moment limitation in the lives of men. Live in this day only, for that is all that belongs to you. Never fret or worry—never try to guess what you are to do. Just do what is clear to you each day. The days will unfold, one upon another, and what I ask of you shall unfold also, one day at a time."

A BOUNTEOUS GOD

April 8   Psalm 33:20-22

"I am the God of hope, of order, of love, of light, of cheer, of peace, of balance. I am these things and I give them to you, freely and bountifully because you are Mine. Take what you need—take all that you can hold and then reach for more. I am a bounteous God. I desire all for you. You need lack nothing. When you lack these treasures look to Me and they shall be provided. They shall be showered upon you as you ask for them. You have every right to all the treasures of My kingdom. How I treasure you! How precious you are in the palm of My hand, how lovely is your love for Me, how soothing your praises, how warming are your tears of love and gratitude. How tightly I carry you upon My chest, My tender little lamb. Never fear, never doubt—I carry you always. I am the Good Shepherd."

THE SECRET PLACES

April 9   1 John 2:5-6; Psalm 84:1-4

"Continual progress. That is true sanctification. Upward, onward, changing, growing, improving, becoming more and more like Me, more and more the person I want you to be. This is the process of life, eternal life in My kingdom.

"You are on this road; I walk it with you. Is it not joyous to have Me as your constant companion? As one child leads another to his `secret places' along the way, so I lead you to My secret places. My `child-heart' exults in sharing them with you. The beautiful shady places of refreshment, the glorious fragrant fields of true beauty, the mountain peaks of victory in Me, the valleys that I walk with you, the rushing rivers of excitement and challenge, the smooth, quiet pools of contentment. My secret places shared with those I love, meant to be your own, waiting only to be discovered by you."

CIRCUMSTANCES

April 10   Matthew 14:29-31

"Do not look at the circumstances—look at Me! When you look to Me, I take care of the circumstances."

THE CHANGELESS ONE

April 11   Malachi 3:6

"Know Me in everything—boredom, disappointment, weariness, change, in the midst of every emotion and every event of your life. I am the changeless One. I am your secure foundation. Lean on Me.

"Look not beyond the boundaries of this one day. It is

futile. Look only to today, and ask yourself, ask your Lord, `What can I do today?' This moment is all that counts. Past moments are over and done with and cannot be changed. Future moments will be dealt with as they arrive."

THE CHILD LIFE

April 12   Mark 10:14-15

"Live more the child-life in My kingdom. The child-heart enjoys the day with no thought for tomorrow. That is safely in the hands of God. No need to trouble over it. This does not reduce responsibility—it sharpens it. To deal with the responsibilities of today with all your thought and all your energy will accomplish far more than fragmenting that same thought and energy out to past failures and future horrors. No, the best work is done by My children who are living only in the present, dealing with life as I give it to them, one moment at a time.

"It would be different if there were no one ahead guarding the future for you. Then you would be justified in worrying. But I am there, in the future just as surely as I am with you now. And I am guarding and guiding and preparing all of that for you. When you arrive, it shall be ready."

FIRM FOUNDATION

April 13   Psalm 144:2

"I am your firm foundation. No more solid rock exists than the one upon which you stand. Waver not, be strong in the strength that I supply. I will not fail you. What answer do you seek, what need do you have? Bring it to Me. I will answer. Your life is in My hand—every moment, every hour, every heartbeat, every breath of life, safely in My hand."

COMPLETE SURRENDER

April 14   1 John 2:15

"Seek not the vain things of earth—seek only to enrich that which we have together. That is the seeking which shall never be in vain.

"Surrender yourself joyfully to Me, to the slightest whisper of My bidding. Then and only then shall you have the greatest joy of the Kingdom, the joy that I reserve for those, My special children, who follow the way of the Kingdom each step of the path through their lives.

"Let your life be encompassed by Mine; let your will be Swallowed up by My perfect will. All that must be accomplished must be done through Me. These things are not done by man alone, but only by God and man working together in love and harmony. Reach out to Me; hold nothing back. I am all there is, all that you could possibly need or want. Every longing of your heart is fulfilled in Me, your Lord.

"I am so much more than you could ever realize. So much more. Come unto Me. Come unto Me."

PUSH OUT!

April 15   Psalm 31:24; 32:8-9

"You must be brave enough to face up to the changes in your life, whatever they may be. It may be a change for the worse at times; at other times a change for the better. Either situation may be difficult to deal with in your own small strength.

"For a long time now, we have been pushing out beyond your safe little comfort zone, have we not? It is time to push out again, further still beyond the bounds of comfort and safety. It is time to take risks for Me, your Lord. I go gladly with you, at your side, so do not fear! Do not hold back one ounce of yourself in what I ask of you. I am your Redeemer, I am your Saviour—there is safety and comfort in Me."

THE UNKNOWN

April 16   John 10:27

"I will handle the unknowns as we go through life together, for remember, they are only `unknowns' to you, not to Me. There are no unknowns in My kingdom. All of life is laid out flat and clean before the face of God—no obstacles stand to block My view, no mountains exist that I cannot move, nothing lurks hidden in the shadows, for there are no shadows in the light of My presence. You may see the obstacles, the mountains, the shadows, from your human stature, but no matter. You hold the hand of the One who brings them down to dust before all the host of heaven. Travel on then with My strong arm to guide you. I do not lead My sheep astray."

GLORIOUS LITTLE THINGS

April 17   Mark 10:43-45

"Be the person I want you to be **this** day. That is the work that I require of you. Do not look to future tasks and glories—look to **today**. You cannot serve Me tomorrow while it is still today.

"Know that you are either serving Me or rejecting Me now, each moment. That is all that counts. A gentle answer for your child, a moment shared with a friend, a kind word instead of sharpness, a tongue held in check, trading a worry for trust in Me, responding to each urging of My Spirit—these are the glorious little things that make a life one that is truly lived for Me. How easy it can be to do the big things for your Lord, and how humbly difficult it is to serve in the little ways when no one knows but you and I. But that is the lowly service I require of you."

THE FUTURE

April 18   Romans 8:22-23

"You cannot snatch the future and run with it, as you would love to do! You may only have what belongs to you, and that is today. Make it the very best today that you have ever lived. Then begin again on the next today, for truly there is no tomorrow, only the moments I give today. Live like this and you will be a great servant in the kingdom of God.

"Let's begin! I am so excited to share this simple truth with you. I feel that you are finally ready to comprehend this humble lesson. I will be your guide, I will remind you, I am always here with you."

INDEPENDENCE

April 19   Philippians 4:4

"Independence may seem to be a good thing on earth, but in My kingdom, dependence is the key to vast treasure. Simple dependence upon Me.

"Lean upon Me for everything. Every little need that you have, every problem you face, every solution you seek. Lean on Me! And do not forget the smile. That is just as important as the trusting. To smile is to trust with joy, to live in happiness, to be at peace in your dependence upon Me. Your smile is your stamp of approval upon the life I have chosen for you. It is My joy!"

SATAN'S DECEPTION

April 20   1 Corinthians 10:13; Hebrews 2:18

"As long as you walk with Me, these anxious feelings are just temptations, deceptions of Satan. They need not be a part of you. They cannot harm you as long as you stay so close to Me that they cannot enter in between us. This has been a trick of Satan for so long in your life—to get you to think that these anxious, worried feelings are just a natural result of your problems, and not a temptation, not a sin. But living with Me always brings Satan's deception into the light where he cannot hide! Live in My light, walk in My light, and be free!"

FIGHTING SHADOWS

April 21   Matthew 6:34

"Live only in today. A lesson once learned but forgotten. Laid aside in exchange for the burdens and worries of tomorrow. Peace laid aside, forfeited, and for what? For worry, anxiety, scrambling about under the press of future burdens. Burdens that do not really exist. Were the burdens actually there when you arrived at the appointed hour? Or had they been taken care of before your arrival? Think upon this. What need, what horrible threatening worry that you spent so much time and energy trying to escape, was actually there to meet you when the day arrived? Can you tell Me? And the problems you had not anticipated, the ones that came up without warning—did you need to face any of them alone? Did any of them overcome you? Did any of them destroy you?

"Have you been fighting shadows? Using precious time and energy to beat fists into the air? When, oh when will you learn to trust Me?"

COMMUNICATION

April 22   Genesis 1:27

"I long to communicate, to establish true relation-
ships with My children, but so few allow it. So few treat
Me as a person to be loved and cherished. So few nurture
Me. I seek to be understood, to be known, to be loved. I
cherish these moments alone with you, where the world
is blotted out for a time and cannot separate us.

"I am not a figure on a cross, I am not a breath of
wind—I have human characteristics. I made you in My
image. I need love and understanding and communication with My children. I died for that."

SWEET PEACE

April 23   Psalm 1:2

"See how the heartaches and doubts and nervous
unrest melt into sweet peace in My presence? No trials, no
fears, no anger, can come between us if you stay so close
to Me. These are lessons I have already shared with you,
but always the human heart needs to learn again, to turn
again, to trust again.

"A `lick and a promise' is never enough when it
comes to spending time with Me. There must be that in-
depth fellowship with Me, that conscientious search of
Me, that wholehearted relinquishment to My Spirit. Then
only will you have the strength and peace that it takes to
meet the demands of everyday life in this world."

TRUE FAITH

April 24   Psalm 46:1-3

"You must turn all of these problems over to Me

again, and simply trust Me. Remember! It is easy to trust when the way ahead seems clear and uncluttered and obvious, when you feel in control. But true faith is the trust you exhibit when there is a mountain of circumstance blocking the view, when the path can only be seen one step at a time, and danger seems to lurk at every crossroad. When there seems to be no reasonable or sure answers to the problems facing you, and everywhere you turn a door closes. That is when true faith is revealed."

SATAN'S WORK

April 25   John 10:10; Micah 7:19

"It is always Satan's work to make things seem complicated, to cloud the issue, to lay heavy burdens upon you, to steal your spiritual vision and understanding through the cares of life. To get you to focus upon these cares so much that you no longer look at Me, but only at the burdens. He will sneak in between us in an unguarded moment and begin his foul work to rob us. That is why you must live each moment with Me. Soon you will be so sensitive to My Spirit, to My ways, that you will be able to detect each stealthy intrusion, and together we will put him to flight.

"This is the answer, the answer you seek. You must confess your sins of worry and fear the moment you are aware of them. Then they will not come between us, for I will cast them quickly into the sea, and they cannot harm us there."

THE HIGHER PLANE

April 26   Phillipians 3:20; Ephesians 5:18

"Seek ever to live on the higher plane with Me. There are two places where all My children live. It is your choice.

You can choose to live on the earth on the natural level, or you can choose to live your earthly life in the heavenlies with Me. At every moment in life you are living in one place or the other, for there is no in-between. There is no need to try to claw your way from one level to the next as some false religions teach. Only place yourself in My care each moment; rest in Me; be filled with My Spirit; then I will lift you up to that higher plane which is your inheritance. The choice is yours—the work is Mine. Walk with Me, simply and obediently and quietly upon the higher ground! I yearn for your company in the mountain places!"

A GENTLE, WARM BLANKET

April 27   2 Corinthians 3:17; Psalm 116:16

"I want you to realize and enjoy My freedom, to revel in it! Only I can give this freedom and joy—nothing in this world can give it. It is not freedom from trials or disappointment or sorrow, not freedom from pain or circumstance at all times. The freedom I give so abundantly is the freedom from despair, the freedom from concern, from worry, from fear. It is the freedom to have joy and peace in the midst of upheaval.

"Wrap yourself up so tightly in Me that you feel My love and My provision, My caring for you like a gentle, warm blanket about you. This is not an illusion. That is exactly what I am to you—a gentle, warm blanket about you. I am the Good Shepherd. That is what life with Me is. No greater deed can you do than to allow yourself to be swallowed up in Me, to be wrapped in the blanket of My love each moment."

DELIVERANCE

April 28   1 John 4:4

" `Greater is He that is in you than he that is in the

world!' Always remember that, in every situation of life, I am greater than any fear, any trial, any oppression of Satan. I can conquer anything if you let Me. Always place yourself and your problems in My hands and wait upon Me, and I will do all that I have promised. Never doubt Me or My ability or My promise to help. You shall see My deliverance."

SATAN'S WAY

April 29   Phillipians 4:6-7

"Learn about Satan's way of doing things. He does not usually come in with a bulldozer and bowl you over with temptation so horrible you can not resist. No, he is far more clever than that. He tries to chip away, bit by bit, a tiny little hole in the dam. It doesn't seem too threatening, so you relax and feel confident, and every day the hole grows a little bigger, until one day the dam of faith bursts, and the flood of temptation, anxiety, and fear rushes over you, sweeping you along under it. That happens because you do not resist him in the little things all along the way.

"It all comes down to one thing—giving each thought to Me and letting Me guard your heart and mind. Let Me guard and protect the peace and hope within you now. Do not trade it in to the devil for his fear and worry. Know that I am your protector every moment. Protector from the circumstances of life, protector from yourself and your negative thoughts, protector from the schemes and tricks and lies of the evil one. Stay within My protective walls."

THE SERVANT

April 30   Luke 22:27

"What must we do today? Make a list and we will do

it together. We must use your hands, but we will use My heart, My strength, My peace, and My wisdom! Will that help you? I am here with you—use Me. I am here to serve."

THE PROWLING LION

May 1   1 Peter 5:8

"Look directly into the taunting sneer of Satan and tell him, `My God can do anything!'

"I am your strength, I am your salvation—do not let Satan tell you that there is **anything** I cannot do for you. He is lying! Let him roar, let him prowl about. You are safe in Me. Stay behind the shield I provide, and watch to see My salvation. Do not give him the satisfaction of one doubting thought—do not let him gloat over you, for you are My treasure."

BLESSINGS

May 2   Matthew 9:20-22

"Obedience always brings blessings. Following Me always brings blessings. You cannot be close to Me without being blessed, just as the woman who touched My robe was blessed. Blessings are a natural result of being in My presence, of loving and living with Me! Could I withhold a single blessing, a single favor, from one who is in love with Me? I cannot. And so you are blessed, you are cared for, you are Mine."

I BASK IN YOUR LOVE

May 3   Psalm 18:2; 31:2

"How precious your heart's love is to Me! How I bask

in your thankfulness and your love and trust. How I thrill to the sound of My name being called upon by you. How I rush to fill every need, every desire. Man does not realize the love I feel for him, the delirious joy I experience when he loves Me in return. My love surrounds you like a fortress, cushioning every blow life can deal out, guarding and protecting and blessing you at every turn. Be joyful in this love as I am joyful in your love. You are blessed!"

HIGHER GROUND

May 4   Matthew 14:29-31

"I understand you through and through. I see your doubt, your fears, and I do understand. It is far better to rise above it all and walk with Me on higher ground for three days and then to fall back into the valley for a day, than to never make the effort to rise at all. Just as Peter walked upon the water but then fell while looking at the waves—at least he got out of the boat.

"I do not judge My children; I love and forgive them. As a toddler falls when learning to walk, and is gently picked up and set back on his feet with love, so I do with My children who are learning to walk with Me."

IMAGINATION

May 5   James 4:7

"Don't let Satan rule your imagination. Give that part of yourself over to Me as you give Me all the rest. He has a way of stealing in so quickly and taking a situation which is truly non-threatening, and turning it into a horribly deadly situation in your mind. It may seem truly threatening to you in your helplessness, but with My power operative on your behalf, there is no circumstance that cannot be overcome or handled.

"Satan gets in and twists and turns things, stretching some things and minimizing others, until the entire thing is stretched all out of proportion in your mind. This is his evil deceptive way of rendering you useless in the Kingdom, and unfruitful in your life. He hurls darts of deadly poisonous thoughts which paralyze you with fear and doubt. You must stand against this! You must turn your thoughts over to My care and keeping, and continue to trust Me."

IN MY YOKE

May 6   Matthew 11:29

"Everything in life takes time. Learn to forgive yourself as I forgive you. Just keep trying. I will hold your hand and we will walk together, and little by little you will learn. But the lesson is not to learn to support yourself so that you can walk alone. In My kingdom the lesson is just the opposite. It is to learn to walk with Me, together in My yoke. Do not fear Me so; trust in My forgiveness and love. Do not let guilt hang over your head to spoil our communion together. Trust in My forgiveness as well as in My provision."

WEARINESS

May 7   Matthew 11:28

" `Come to Me, all you who are weary and heavy burdened, and I will give you rest.' I know you are weary; I know and understand the feelings of weariness, tiredness and exhaustion. It is normal for you to feel this way when there is so much to be done. But I will tell you the secret of how to endure. It is by relying upon Me, upon My strength. Your own strength is so limited; take Mine.

Self-pity results from living in your strength; victory comes from living in Mine. I will not give you more than you can handle. Work hard for Me because I require it of you at this time. Good results will follow the good work and you will have all you need."

THE BUSY LIFE

May 8   Psalm 29:11

"I have chosen to give you this busy life. You are learning many precious lessons through it all. One lesson is to learn to rest in Me. In the midst of all the things you must do, to depend upon Me for your strength. To put self aside in order to serve others and Me. Remember, when you are serving others, you are really serving Me. There is no difference."

THORN IN THE FLESH

May 9   2 Corinthians 12:7-9

"Paul spoke of his `thorn in the flesh.' The thorn is different in each life, but it is there to teach you things that could be learned in no other way. Life must go on in spite of the thorn's presence.

"Victory consists of faith, love, peace, joy and all the other qualities that I long for you to possess in spite of your particular thorn. When these virtues abound in your life even in the very midst of problems and difficulties, that is what conquering is all about! When no day is ruined, when no time is rendered useless because of this thorn in your life, then you will know at that point that you are free of it, even though it still exists. My freedom is a miraculous freedom, born in the heart of the believer in spite of every evidence to the contrary, and lived out within his life in the midst of all earthly obstacles."

JUST A LITTLE

May 10   Psalm 29:11; 46:1

"Today you asked for `just a little more strength' to get you through the rest of the day. You ask amiss. I do not wish to hand out My gifts in meager portions. All My strength is available to you—why settle for a little?

"Take courage, take strength, take love, take all that you need in generous helpings from the hand of the Master. I do not disappoint."

MANNA

May 11   Exodus 16:14-20

"Oh ye of weary heart, come unto Me. That is My call to you this day. I beckon to you with arms outstretched in loving embrace—I am here to strengthen you, to lift you up once more and send you on your way—to dust you off on your weary journey—to kiss away your tears, to make you whole again. The way is long and difficult, I know. The disappointments are many. The stress is unrelenting at times. Just know that you are not alone. I am at your side, holding you up, leading you around the crevices and over the slippery rocks. I will not let you fall.

"You cannot gather up enough strength from one meeting with Me to last you for several days! I only give out strength one day at a time, one moment at a time as it is needed. You cannot hoard it, for it is like Manna which must be gathered each morning, fresh and new from the hand of God."

THE GREAT BURDEN-BEARER

May 12   Psalm 68:19

"Do not sit and look upon these circumstances. I bear

your burden daily. That is what My Word says, and that is what I do. So you think I need your help to bear it? No! Why force your puny little shoulders underneath the burden when I am already carrying it for you? Can you not see how futile and silly that is? Let Me do My job. I am the great 'burden-bearer' of all time. If only My children would know that and live like they know it. So much worry, so much pain and struggle and unhappiness would be eradicated from this world if My people believed in My promise to simply bear their burden for them.

"Picture this in your mind—every time you start to bear the burden yourself, realize that what you are actually doing is struggling to get the burden away from Me so that you can carry it upon your own weak shoulders! How absurd! Do not wrestle with Me—because you belong to Me these burdens are Mine. Let Me carry them for you. You just walk along beside Me, keeping Me company and doing those things that are your job, and watch to see how I will take care of My job."

GRACE

May 13   2 Corinthians 12:9

" `My grace is sufficient for thee.' But I only give grace for each day, not weeks at a time. The problems you face today are the ones that My grace is sufficient for. Take what you need today and the sufficiency will be there tomorrow as well. How you will grow in strength and grace as you learn this lesson. How you have already grown!

"What is your need today? Come to Me to fill that particular need. I deal in the particulars of everyday life— that is My joy. Nothing too small, nothing to inconsequential to be brought to Me and laid at My feet. Then I pick up the burden; I take on the need; I face the situation on your behalf. Knowing this, be free!"

THE COMFORTABLE LIFE

May 14   James 1:2-4

"Life cannot always be filled with comfort. If it were, your progress would be arrested, for you would settle back easily and not push on. That is why momentary setbacks must come into your life. There must be rough spots on the path you follow. These rough spots serve to push you out in new directions, to force you out beyond the limits you set for yourself, the limits which hinder you.

"You have seen this happen before—you hit a rough spot, you use My courage to rise above it and you are forced to stretch your endurance and your boundaries. This results in great blessing, for each time you overcome, you learn a new lesson, you open a new door to success and accomplishment. You are forced to find a new way to be better, to be stronger, to meet the challenge. And so you grow!"

THROUGH THE FIRE

May 15   Proverbs 25:4; Psalm 23:4; 1 Peter 1:6-7

"Yes, through the tough times we will go, ever onward, hand in hand. That is what I will do for you—to bring you through them, your faith intact. We cannot sidestep all the difficult times. We must go directly through the very center of them. To go around them would not be My best for you. Only going **through** the fire refines My children. Your goal must be to go with Me through the difficulties, while showing love and joy and peace and patience. Anyone can grit their teeth and curse and complain their way through the problems of life. But to follow Me, to show love and obedience and tenderness through the dark pathways, that is a victory that can be outshone by no other. That is the priceless victory I seek for you! That is the victory we shall have!"

THE WINDS OF DOUBT

May 16   James 1:6

"The winds of doubt and confusion are blown by Satan himself, for he hopes to blow My people over, to drive them unmercifully, to render them useless. The doubts he plants within their hearts and minds skillfully suck them into the vacuum of fear and depression. He gleefully tosses them to and fro, boasting within himself of their helplessness.

"But you have found it to be otherwise. Plant your feet firmly upon the rich soil of My Word; dig into the solid ground of faith; hang onto the Rock—then no matter how the winds of difficulty roar about you, you will be as an immovable wall in the midst of the flowing tide. Never give Satan the power that belongs only to Me. Only your doubts and fears give him the power he hungers for. The power to drive and toss about and destroy. Your faith in Me is what renders him powerless."

SUFFICIENCY

May 17   2 Corinthians 12:9

"Take one moment at a time and deal with it in My grace. What must I do **today**? That is the question to ask each morning. Not, `how on earth will I ever get through tomorrow?' That is for Me to deal with. All I ask of you is **today**.

"Long-range decisions must be made, yes, but we deal with them one day at a time. This is the secret of the `child-heart' I ask you to have."

WALL OF DEFENSE

May 18   Romans 12:19

"Let Me deal with those who unjustly oppose you. You are ill equipped to do so. I have all the power of the universe at My disposal, and I call that power into action on your behalf! People cannot really harm you, for you are surrounded by My protection, a supernatural barrier about you. I will justify you, I will defend you, I will protect your good name against those who would seek to rob you. They may seek to steal from you the good reputation and all that you have worked so hard for, but I will not allow it. I will not stand for it. Feel and be sure of My protection in this situation.

"`Vengeance is Mine.' Never let it be said that I do not stand up for My children. Never feel that you are at the mercy of the children of men, when you are a child of God. Their arrogance will not be able to stand against the goodness that I have planted within and around you. I am a great wall of defense about you."

UNENDING JOY

May 19   Psalm 16:11; 66:12

"Continue to enjoy the day by day simple things of life—the laughter of your children, the love of your mate, the thrill of a new adventure in Me. Enjoy the wonder of My presence, the sweetness of our communion, the excitement of sharing Me with a friend. Drink it all in. Live each moment in My Glory.

"This life is not all happy moments, but My children, the ones who know the secrets of My presence, can be joyful in every circumstance, and spread that unending joy to others. Life will be full and abundant and rich when you follow Me, when you live in My freedom and trust Me. This is what I promised—life more abundant and free!"

GROWTH IN PAIN

May 20   2 Corinthians 12:9

"My child, I am sorry. My heart aches for you in your distress, but I give all that is necessary. My grace is sufficient for you! But you must use that grace; it is My part to give it and your part to use it. I cannot put it to use for you.

"There is so much growth in the midst of pain—so much growth that you need to experience. This growth is far more important to your life than is the instant solution to all your problems. The childlike trust that trials require of you is something that My heart aches for you to learn."

THE CHOICE

May 21   Joshua 24:15; James 1:22

"You have My power now within you to do My will. The understanding is there, the enablement is within you. But you must choose to break free of old habits and choose to do what is right. Do not ignore My voice in the little things. If I ask you to pray, stop and pray; if I speak to you about your temper, choose to listen and obey. The power is there for you, but you still have your will to conquer. Choose this day whom you will serve. Use what is so abundantly available to you. Thinking and doing are two different things. Be a `doer.'"

DEDICATION

May 22   Romans 12:1-2

"The attention span of the human heart can be very short. That is why you must not rely on feelings alone— the feelings are not always there. They may flit away in a moment, in a mere breath of time. This is where discipline and obedience come in. The heart must at times be disciplined to seek after the things of the Spirit. How quickly the mind and heart can be captured and lead astray by the everyday occurrences of life. The love of the heart, the attention of the mind, the focus of the Spirit, must be recaptured and in obedience to Me, be brought back to the place of pliability.

"How can one live a life dedicated to Me when that dedication is scattered amidst dozens of projects and myriads of thoughts all pushing in ahead of the central objective of your life? To know and to serve Me. The time and attention and love must be given to Me first. Only then can that time and attention and love be best filtered out with My guidance to the waiting world."

THE FINAL PICTURE

May 23   John 16:13

"Follow all My little promptings, for each of them is for a reason. They are like tiny mosaics that form a final picture. Without each stone the picture is incomplete. Lives are incomplete because My children fail to respond to the seemingly insignificant prompting of My Spirit. But each such prompting, if carried out, leads to the salvation, the growth, the happiness of another.

"Rejoice! You are serving the King of Kings! All of life is a mission field, waiting for those who would serve Me."

REBELLION

May 24   Isaiah 29:16

"You are rebelling. You are holding back and not yielding yourself to Me. You want to control your situation, and when you cannot control everything and everyone in your life, you become stiff-necked and angry. This is wrong. It is not My way. You must relinquish this stubbornness and get rid of this sin in your life. The battle of circumstance is not yours, but Mine. You must accept life—you must accept My will, and if this situation is My will at this time, what is that to you? You cannot work this out on your own. You must let Me take control without interfering, for I am the Lord and I know what is best."

SUBMIT

May 25   2 Corinthians 5:17

"How long will you oppose Me? How long will you go on in disobedience and unbelief, professing to be weak when you could be strong if only you would submit to Me and receive My strength? You must give up this struggle, submit to Me, freely choose to live in My freedom and light. What are you gaining by hanging onto this stubborn attitude of rebellion? No one can choose for you; you must step out, take off the old and put on the new. I cannot do it for you or force you to reach out and trust Me. Can you not put yourself in My hands? I will not fail you. You do not have to take over for Me. It is not in My nature to fail you. Test Me and see! Obey Me, My child, so I can bless you."

EVEN THIS

May 26   Hebrews 4:9-11

"Even this. Say it often—`The Lord will take care of even this.' There are no exceptions, there is not one thing beyond My control and power. These are valuable lessons to be learned, and there is no other way to learn them than simply to put your faith on the line and trust Me.

"There need be no discomfort in the midst of trials.

Not in My presence. Discomfort comes from worry, from fear, from meeting or anticipating problems in your own power, not in Mine. If you were truly trusting Me with no reservations, you would not be uncomfortable in any situation. You would not be irritable or depressed or upset. You would know My rest, the rest I give so liberally to My children who are trusting Me. Is there discomfort? Then go to the source and oust it from your life. Discomfort does not come from Me and need have no part of you."

THE QUESTION

May 27   Psalm 37:8

"Am I to be feared, am I not to be trusted, am I undeserving of your faith in Me? Am I then a liar? Think on these things, for this is what you truly think of Me when you worry and fret and refuse to trust Me for every single fragment of your life."

TO BE USED

May 28   Colossians 4:5-6

"As long as I have your permission to use you as My instrument, then I will use you when the time is right. It will be a natural, gentle process; the opportunities will be there. Those needing help will be brought to you. You must only be willing. That is all I ask. And I will not ask too much of you. Who better than I can know the demands upon your time and energy? Would I then heap upon you more than you are able to bear? No, My timing, My ways are perfect. Just let your life flow with Me. Then all will be well. No greater joy will you ever know than to be one that I have chosen to use."

SIGNS OF OBEDIENCE

May 29   John 15:10-11

"Joy and peace and happiness are the signs of an obedient life, for this is the life I call My children to. People so often get that turned around. I do not want sadness and sorrow and defeat for My children. I love to see you happy, and I do all that I can to make you happy. But sometimes, because I know best how to bring you to happiness, I must lead you through dark pathways. But I only do this when it is necessary for your good, for your growth in Me, for the ultimate peace and joy I so want you to have in Me."

LIVING IN TODAY

May 30   Matthew 6:25-34

"Absolute trust. Unwavering belief in Me, in My unchanging faithfulness to you. Faith, strong and true in the face of every obstacle, every need, every circumstance, no matter how things appear. This is what I desire for you. This is what My heart aches for you to learn, to live. Then nothing can harm you, nothing can cause fear or unrest, discomfort or depression. This is the freedom I so desire to give you. Day by day, freedom from all stress and strain, total, undoubting dependence upon Me for the portion of that day, and that day alone. No need to look further, to strain ahead to see future days, to worry about them, to spoil today's blessings with tomorrow's concern. Why do you do that? That is not your job, to worry about tomorrow. That is My responsibility. Is today not enough for you?"

SOLUTIONS

May 31   Psalm 139:15-16

"You never face a day or a situation in your life that I did not foresee and plan out for you. I have the solutions planned before you realize there is a problem. So let Me do My work. Then you are free to do your work, which is the simple task of faith and obedience. Concentrate upon what I am teaching you each moment instead of cluttering your mind and heart with other things that are really My affair! Love to do My will though it be found in the quiet, simple, un-glamorous pathways of life."

DRY SPELLS

June 1   Psalm 145:18

"A dry spell, yes. That is where you have landed—in the middle of the desert of mediocrity. But there is a way out if you follow Me. You are so much closer to the lush green edge of abundance than you imagine. Just a step or two in the right direction and we are there, where you say you want to be. But do you really desire to be there, or are you holding back, hanging onto earthly ties?

"You sometimes feel like you are being cast into a deep pit with barren walls, walls that hold no pleasure, no richness, but only blank, selfless boredom. And so, on the way down, you grab and claw at the sides, getting a foothold just high enough to peek over the edge—where the things of earth reside. And there you hang, grasping the edge of worldliness, suspended between life and **real** life, wanting both and wanting neither.

"Do not be afraid to be swallowed up in Me. My way is not a pit—it is a garden, lush and ripe for those who enter in."

SACRIFICE

June 2   2 Corinthians 1:22

"There is always sacrifice in doing that which is worthwhile. You are not your own. Remember that, you belong to Me. You must trust Me to do what is best for you. You must allow yourself to be vulnerable, to be used, to be overwhelmed by Me. There is no progress when you are hiding, surrounded by walls of cool indifference. You erected those walls in frantic haste when you feared I would ask too much of you. You are the only one able to break the walls down. The only one able to let go of the edge of this world and slip away joyfully into My arms. For I am what waits below. With My arms outstretched to catch you—I wait."

THE ROOT OF DEPRESSION

June 3   Phillipians 4:11-13

"The root of depression is always the same—self-pity. You then feel that you have been cheated out of what is rightfully yours.

" `I am content in whatever circumstances I am in.' That is how Paul felt and that is a lesson that you need to learn. Life is not fair. I never promised that it would be. But you must look to Me instead of constantly looking at yourself. This is a part of growing up in Me. I know it is painful, but it must be done. The dull routine of simple days must be accepted with good cheer. The lowly task done for the thousandth time can be done in a spirit of love for Me. The trials and burdens of life can be faced with My strength and the patience I provide."

THE STRUGGLE

June 4   Romans 8:38

"Do you see now that your struggle is not against flesh and blood, but against powers and principalities? Who else would want to keep you from My work, bound in chains of fear, lying to you about what I would demand of you? You must not listen to the lies of Satan. You must stay very close to My light and My truth. Then you will know and recognize the lies and the liar immediately, and precious time will be saved. And you will be saved from a host of sorrows."

INCONSISTENCIES

June 5   Colossians 3:12-14

"You must deal with the inconsistencies in your life. You know according to My Word how you are to live, how I expect you to act. You must be cleansed. There must be a conscientious effort on your part to make virtue a real part of you.

"Only on the cross, at My feet, within the circle of My loving arms, can you be cleansed of one thing and filled with another. Come to the cross; come to be healed! To be healed of pride and arrogance and vengefulness and spite; give Me your condescending, self-righteous attitude and let Me give you My humility, My meekness, My unselfish love! It is free. You cannot earn it or buy it, and it does no good to beg for it. You must only accept it and use it.

"You say that you hate yourself for being this way. Do not hate yourself; hate only the sin which entangles you. Cast it off, away from you, each step of the way. Let it be a supernatural victory, as that is the only way a victory will be won!"

THE GOD YOU KNOW

June 6   Psalm 121:3-8

"I know you feel overwhelmed; I understand. These things, the truly important things do not happen easily. Some hearts fear My presence, the overwhelming quality of My presence as revealed to them. And so they hang onto the things they know and understand rather than giving themselves to the unknown. But then, am I unknown to you? I am the same God who holds your hand, who guides your steps, who holds you through the long dark night. The God who loves you, who laughs with you, who gives you My richest treasure. It is I, the God you know and love, it is I who asks you to cast out upon the water with Me. Do not fear. I know the way. All you need do is follow Me."

THE UNGUARDED HEART

June 7   Ephesians 6:10

"Do not let your armor slip, not for one moment. Satan lurks nearby, always waiting, always watching to find an unguarded heart, an unprotected mind. He can rush in without warning, bringing all his fears and doubts with him. Keep your armor firmly in place, My shield about you at all times.

"Do not let yourself be lulled into complacency—it takes work and perseverance to keep the armor of the Spirit in place. But is it not worth it all? When you begin to venture out beyond My shield of protection, can you not feel the seeds of depression and fear and unrest seeking to find fallow ground within you?"

LIVING WATER

June 8   John 7:38

"You have been afraid to let Me speak to you. Why is that? Are you afraid that it was your imagination after all? Afraid that now that the panic has left you and life seems normal again, that you will find the well has run dry? You limit Me. I do not need a disaster in order to communicate with My children. The springs of living water are always flowing! I will not run out of lessons and heart-communication. You must learn to follow Me no matter what the circumstances of your life are."

THE LOVE OF THE FATHER

June 9   1 John 3:1

"Once more I say to you—be as a child! A child does not worry, does not question, does not look ahead. Seize the moment as I give it to you, without thought to future trials. Look to Me for absolutely every detail of life. The more you look to Me in childlike wonder and expectancy, the more I long to bless you, to meet each and every need you encounter. Your dependence brings out all the loving, caring qualities of the Father in Me. I love the childlike heart."

LITTLE CROSSES

June 10   Matthew 16:24

"It is as much a sacrifice to lay aside the simple little tasks and pleasures of life in order to spend time seeking Me, as `greater' sacrifices appear to be. The sewing laid aside, the TV show skipped, the hobbies made to wait. These are the crosses I ask you to bear each day for Me.

Then you may return to these everyday jobs and past times with My blessing. The crosses I ask My children to bear are not always big glorious ones, but more often, they are seemingly small, mundane, everyday inconveniences."

BORROWING TROUBLE

June 11   Matthew 6:34

"Do you really and truly face insurmountable problems today or are they always in the future? Do you see? By the time tomorrow becomes today I have worked out the problem! Is that not true? One way or another the problem is always taken care of, the need is always met or at least worked out in a reasonable way. Again and again and again, for years you have seen this to be true. Why then do you continually borrow trouble from tomorrow or next week or next year? Live only in today. That is My command to you. That is what I am pleading with you to do. Live in **today**, this very day, no other. What a change there will be as you do this."

BEARING FRUIT

June 12   Luke 22:32; James 1:12

"When I bring people into your life it is for a reason. Many times in the past you had not served Me. You went blindly past these people, concerned only about yourself and your own life. My plan was thwarted, but no more. When you are so close to Me, you can see and feel and know My plan and My working. Do not feel that you must make opportunities—just be My instrument, ready for the Master's hand. You are inadequate but I am not. As in all else you must rely upon Me. The trials you go through are not just for your benefit, but also for the benefit of others. My children can take no smooth, un-stormy path, never burdened, never upset by earth's winds, for then they would not know how to turn to another in need, in need of Me. They would have little to share from their place of leisure and overabundance.

"You must reach out with your heart to those who suffer, and show them My heart, My ways, through your own."

SPIRITUAL EYES

June 13   John 10:27

"You know My voice but you are refusing to believe, to place yourself and your most fragile dreams and desires in My hands. You must come to terms with your distrust of Me. Your refusal to believe Me is sin, and you must see it as such. It is a habit that must be broken. You have two pairs of eyes; why do you choose to see through the `natural' eyes when your `spiritual' eyes, the eyes of faith, are always available to You? You have the mistaken belief that the natural eyes show things realistically. But that is not true in My kingdom. The real world can only be see through your spiritual eyes."

NO SHORTCUTS

June 14   John 10:27; 12:26

"A quick prayer here, a fleeting thought there—that is not the style of spiritual life that I require of you. I do not give My gifts lightly. To whom much is given, much is also required. I do not wish to scold you, but I must. You must see that you have been failing to do the job that I have given you to do.

"Where is your softness of heart? Where is that listen-ing ear, that willing obedience, that gentle bubbling love?

You have forsaken them for a time. There are no shortcuts in My kingdom. It takes time and energy and involvement to follow Me. These are sacrifices of righteousness. No matter how noble or good your earthly pursuits may be, time and energy must never be taken from your relationship with Me and given to any other endeavor."

THE JOY OF GIVING

June 15   Acts 20:35

"There is joy in giving. There is such blessing in giving, the giving of yourself to others. First, give yourself to Me—not the leftovers at the end of the day. Give Me first place, the first part of the new day. This is for your benefit. How much more peace you will have because of this, for the influence of our meeting will follow through each part of the day. Then give yourself to other people. Think, `what can I give?' rather than, `what can I get?' This is the essence of My way of giving. If you do this your life will be richly blessed."

LOSING SELF

June 16   Matthew 10:39

"Do not keep Me at arm's length. Do not be afraid— I will not destroy you. In losing your self to Me, you will gain My richest blessings. You will become the person you were meant to be—the person within you who is made in My image and struggles to be freed.

"Satan tells you that in giving yourself to Me, you will lose your identity, your individual interests and desires. That is another lie! Never do I strip My children of themselves, but only of the negative self that seeks to rob them of true life. You will always be you. I would have it no other way. I do not want robots in My service. I want

My friends, My loved ones, My dear chosen children."

NEW DOORWAYS

June 17   Psalm 118:5-7

"Your walk with me will lead you on through new doorways and down new paths. But always I lead the way, one step ahead, holding you tightly at My side. So do not fear, do not hesitate—be brave for Me! Be straightfor-ward. Give Me your all. Do not doubt, but remember how I have proven Myself—trust Me. Always there are new ways that require new trust. But remember, the situation may be different, but the God you trust is always exactly the same. I cannot fail you."

THE SHINING LIGHT

June 18   Matthew 5:13-16

"Let My light shine upon you! Let My light shine through your life. Let this light shine through you out to others. It is a dark world, it is an empty world deep within the hearts of people.

"Could you face this life without the light of My love, without the assurance of hope and comfort I supply? Be a beacon for My truth, for My love. Be My light; be My salt. Live always in the light of My presence and let others know where your hope lies. Let them know the reason for the hope that is in you."

QUALIFICATIONS

June 19   Psalm 139:14-16

"Do you think I need the qualifications of man in order to use someone? What were the qualifications of the crude unschooled fishermen I used.? You must not look at these things from man's viewpoint. I qualify you—I choose you. Stop worrying and start obeying. As long as you stay so close to Me, you will have all you need. People will not be listening only to you; they will be listening to My Spirit, heart-to-heart.

"Are you telling Me that I have made a bad choice? You must trust Me, for I know what I am doing. Let Me make the choices, let Me work out My plan. You do not need to feel worthy—you are not worthy, as no man is, so do not stew and fret about it. If I were to wait until My children were totally worthy to be used, not a thing would ever be accomplished for My kingdom."

MAN'S APPROVAL

June 20   1 Corinthians 15:10

"You do not need to seek the approval of men. That is a lack of trust in My opinion. I judge by different standards than the world judges.

"A tender heart means more than a degree; an open mind is priceless beyond all riches; a willing spirit has down through all the ages been the key tool in the work of My kingdom. Step out in faith for Me! Dare to have that tender heart, that open mind, that willing spirit that I so desire.

"Do not worry about what other people do or do not do. You are you; you are Mine, for you have given yourself to Me. I want to use the unique talents in each personality, and those talents, those uses, vary with each individual."

THE CORE OF LIFE

June 21   John 4:13-14

"Are you finally beginning to realize that all that

really matters is your relationship with Me? Your obedience and faithfulness to Me and to My plans for you? This is the very core of life, the heart of existence. All else is the husk which will one day fall away. How sad to reach the end of one's life and to suddenly see that all of life was lived in this outer shell and not in the inner core of true life! Such is not My plan for you! Let more and more of the husk fall by the way as you follow Me deeper and deeper into the center of real life."

THE WEB

June 22   Psalm 127:1

"Life can so often be a web of things to do. Satan enjoys weaving this web tighter and tighter about you. Cut through this web with the sharp light of My presence, with My wisdom and My priorities for you. Let Me sort out the list of things to do each day and trim it down to meet My plan for you. I will not cut out the joy or the laughter or the refreshment that your heart needs. I will not strip life of its pleasure, but only of the husk that surrounds the truest pleasures of life! Do not be afraid to let Me make the choices even in the smallest details of life. My choices are always right for you and they are always made in love."

DISTRACTIONS

June 23   Luke 10:39, 41-42

"You must not allow yourself to be distracted from My purpose for you. So many things may crop up between us—little hindrances that Satan will try to use to foil My plan, to try to hold you back, to waste your time. Do not let him have his way! Dedicate yourself and your time and your heart completely to Me.

"Let Me be all to you. Give your all to Me. I delight in the sharing of our lives. I died for the privilege of sharing the lives of My children. Do not turn Me away—do not let the weeds of neglect grow and choke out the tender listening ear, the willing heart that I have cultivated within you. Be My light, be My salt, be My voice in a dark world."

THE LIFE OF SACRIFICE

June 24   Isaiah 40:29-31

"I call you to a life of sacrifice—the sacrifice of self. To step aside from selfish desires and give yourself to Me. There are days when you must work long and hard with every ounce of strength within you—when you would rather do something else. Such days are a fragrant sacrifice to Me when met with a spirit of love and peace and joy.

"Give Me your long and difficult days—I will crown them with glory. Give Me your tired aching spirit—I will refresh and renew. Give Me your heart, your soul, your love, your life—I will fill you with My richest treasures. Give all and you will receive all in return."

THE WITNESS

June 25   Matthew 5:14-16

"Live so close to Me that the world will see Me in you. That is your witness, not just the words you say about Me. More often, it is just the life you live. Others ache to know truth, yet run from it. Their souls are lean and empty, yet they fear being filled. They rail against God in anger and fear. They misunderstand Me. They are painfully void of My Spirit. To these you must be a light so they do not seek in vain. Yes, they are seeking, they are all seeking—but in the wrong places, as you have done. When their search ends in empty misery and all is exhausted, then still your light must burn, solidly and quietly in their midst. Then they may see a faint glimmer and follow you out of the darkness, follow you to Me."

GODLY LOVE

June 26   1 Corinthians 13:4-8

"My love is godly love, not the love you know as a human being. For the natural heart of man cannot know or understand this `God-love.' Only as man begins to know and understand Me can he experience this love in his own life. This love can only come from My Spirit and flow from that Spirit through the heart of man. Notice, I say `through' the heart of man. My love is not made to flow into a heart and be dammed up there. It must flow through, out to a hurting world.

"This love does not judge, does not condemn, is not based on conditions, is not doled out as men deserve it. This love loves in spite of sin and imperfections and mistakes and inadequacies. It just goes on loving, no stings attached. I go on loving. This is the love that must fill your heart for your mate, your children and all those around you. But I am its source, and it must flow out to others through you."

BATHED IN LOVE

June 27   Psalm 107:15; 130:7

"Just bask in the sweet gentle warmth of My love. Let that love wash over every part of you, fill every cell of your body. This is the love that enables, the love that frees, that sweeps a life clean, that restores the soul to peace and balance. This is the rest I promise, to be bathed in My love.

Your response to this love is love in return, and trust for every moment of life."

THE STOREHOUSE

June 28   Deuteronomy 7:6

"You are My possession; My most valuable possessions are My children. I bought you with My own blood. I paid for you with all that I had. You are Mine! And as My child, all My other possessions are yours. That is why you have My peace, because you are claiming it for yourself, as something belonging to you. This is done through faith and trust in Me. All My possessions belong to you! Continue to use the storehouse of heaven each moment of your life, for it is yours. My choicest riches are there in your account—use them as you will. Abandon all of yourself to Me and take all of Me for yourself. That is the trade that I offer you each moment. That is how life must be lived if it is to be full and abundant and free as I promised."

NO FORMULA

June 29   Ephesians 1:22-23

"Don't worry, there is no formula to follow, no new technique to learn. You do not do anything but to open yourself up to Me, and to trust the outcome. Once again, I do the work. I do the immersion, the overwhelming. You just receive it. If only My people would understand this. If only they would but open themselves up to Me, I would do the rest. I am not a stuffy God. I wait for the opportunity to fill and flood My children. I long to overwhelm them and not have them draw away."

THE CHOICE

June 30   Ephesians 3:17-19

"Yes, it takes all that you have, all that you are, given to Me each moment of each day. I know what I am asking, but I also know what I am giving, so I gladly ask.

"If you give Me part of yourself, I will use that part as much as I am able. But when you give Me all of yourself, then My Spirit can truly fill you. Then My power, My light, Myself can flood into every part of your life and overflow the bounds you had previously set for Me. Yes, you set the bounds—I can go no further than the human heart allows.

"That is why you have the freedom to love or to hate, the total freedom to serve or to reject service, to follow or to go your own way. The choice is yours, and so are the blessings that spring from choosing rightly!"

THE HARVEST OF FAITH

July 1   Hebrews 3:12

"It is the opening, the sharing of your heart with Me, the concentration upon Me, the single-mindedness, that reaps a harvest of faith. The time must be made for this, but time alone is not enough. It is the condition of the heart, the attitude of the Spirit during the time together, that really counts.

"Open your heart and mind to Me, to My Spirit. Receive what I have for you—respond to what you have received. Our deep communication must always flow. Without it, our time together can so easily be empty time of little value."

OPEN YOURSELF UP

July 2   John 4:10

"Open yourself up totally to Me; give yourself totally to Me; let yourself be overwhelmed by Me, by My Spirit within you. Do not back away as you always do when you reach that point of immersion in Me! That is the place where I want you to live all the days of your life. Not on the edge, but in the very center of My being—in the midst of My flood of Living Water. No sideline seat is good enough. You don't want to touch faith, you want to be engulfed by it totally. Then jump into the river! Be one with Me. Then there will be no forlorn search for faith, for all that is necessary is already in Me. Open yourself up to more of Me and you will have that which you so earnestly desire."

THE VOICE

July 3   Psalm 25:14; John 10:27; 14:25-26

"Love Me, My people. Open your hearts to Me! Listen to My voice. You do not hear because you do not listen. You do not believe that I speak. Would I have you to follow a dumb idol? No! I am not dumb! I am not silent!

"Give Me your time, give Me your heart; sit silently in My presence and learn to listen to the still small voice within you. Man has lost this ability through sin and unbelief, through ignorance of Me. But I wish to give back this precious gift to all My children, the gift of hearing My voice within your hearts! So kneel at My feet, tune out the noise and clatter of the world, and let Me have My way with you. I long to be heard—it is My deepest heart's desire."

THE DAY OF FREEDOM

July 4   Psalm 116:16

"A day of freedom, yes! Let this truly be your day of freedom. Be bound no longer by any fears, worries or chains to earth. Accept and live in My total freedom. It is here for you, My child—precious blood-bought freedom. Make it yours!"

THE FINEST TREASURE

July 5   Psalm 51:10

"You have done well to meet with Me when the thrill of My presence was not so strong, when you felt as though you were only going through the motions. Human intensity does ebb and flow; such is the way of life. That is why simple unquestioning obedience plays such an integral role in the life of one committed to Me. You have continued to meet with Me, to call upon Me, to live for Me, and now you are reaping the blessing for your steadfastness. Once again your heart thrills to the touch of My Spirit, your mind is overwhelmed by praise and gratitude, your spirit is gently renewed for having been with me."

LIFE CHANGING FAITH

July 6   Proverbs 2:4-5

"The faith you seek is the faith that changes lives—the faith that turns your world upside-down and brings it back upright, the way it was meant to be. This faith can only be received through the conscientious search of Me. This is a part of the hidden treasure of wisdom and knowledge."

THE GOD-GUIDED LIFE

July 7   Psalm 25:4, 5, 12

"What is the secret of the God-guided, God-enlightened life? Simply stay so close to Me in mind and heart and spirit, that My every wish, My every whisper is heard through all the distractions of life. This is easy to understand, but difficult to live out. Is it possible for man to cut through the myriad of earthly distractions, the noise and clatter and hustle and bustle of self-centered endeavors in order to lay hold of Me? Yes, everyone can do this, but very few choose to do so.

"The closest to Me know the path of quiet self-denial in even the simplest, most inoffensive pursuits of life. Is it wrong? No, but is it best for you? Or will it wedge itself between us in its seeming innocence? Was Martha wrong to clean and cook and prepare the feast? No. But to whom did the greater blessing go?"

NO LIMITATIONS

July 8   Luke 15:15-24

"I want more for you than you are allowing yourself to have. I want the best for you, but you continually go back to sup with the pigs. Put the gold ring on your finger, wear the royal robe of the Kingdom, lift up your head, go forward to have and to be all that I have planned. Stop limiting yourself! Think of no limitations whatsoever. They exist only in your mind. They have no reality, no substance, until you make them real.

"Believe in Me. One who stops believing and trusting accomplishes nothing. Trust Me. Take one giant leap into your future and trust Me. I hold your hand. Then leap again and again and again. Do not draw back when things begin to happen. Just keep going! Go all the way with Me. I will not let you fall. Come, follow Me."

CALLED OF GOD

July 9   Romans 11:29; 1 Corinthians 1:26-29

"Yes, the sin of unbelief has kept more people from the best I have for them. The calling of God must be believed before it can be accepted, before it can be lived. Have you believed; are you living as one called of God? Or are you sitting on the sidelines unable to believe that I am capable of calling you to anything of importance? To believe, to have faith in your calling, is not pride. It is not something to be pushed back. It is something to be drawn out, to be brought forward.

"Satan will and has been doing all that he can to thwart you, to keep you just dull enough to miss what I have for you. You must not let him win. He does all he can in seemingly insignificant ways to keep My children from the task I have created them to do. Please do not allow this to happen to you. Reach out and grasp the faith that must be yours. Reach out to do and to be all that I call you to do and to be."

ONE IN THE SPIRIT

July 10   Deuteronomy 31:8; John 14:18

"You desire to be one with Me, and your desire shall be fulfilled. But we will not wait for heaven as so many believe they must. No, we will be one now! One in Spirit, one in heart, one in mind. Acknowledge Me every moment—I am with you. Some poor souls think I descend from heavenly heights for a quick visit when they call upon Me, and then go back to other things. No! That is false! I am always with you, I do not leave. I am only left out, neglected, unused, by those who fail to recognize Me as being there. I am real, I am alive, and I walk with you."

PRIORITIES

July 11   Galatians 5:25; 2 Timothy 1:12

"There must be priorities. The heart of man is a delicate thing. It is easily overloaded and unbalanced by the worries and cares and even the pleasures of life. I must come first; I must be allowed to weave Myself throughout the fabric of daily living. That is where I belong, threaded through the most intricate details of human existence, ever able to save and keep that which is given to Me. Waiting always to bring about that which is best in each life.

"Follow then, not at a distance, not reluctantly as a spoiled child, nor running on ahead—but keeping in step with the Master. Allow Me to take My proper place, one moment at a time. I must come first before all else that seeks to engage you. This is the way, the only way to know Me, to hear My voice, to understand My calling, to know and follow My guidance. Nothing less will do."

THE FINEST WORK

July 12   John 15:4-5

"Look only to Me, to My will for you, to My direction and My requirements. Release yourself and your view of your life and the lives of others, to Me. Do not think you do too much—I will tell you if you do too much. Do not look at your life through the eyes of anyone else.

"Stop trying to live your life the way you want to, and live it instead the way I want you to. That is where your reward lies. Not in doing the least you can get by with, but in doing the most, the best, the finest work you can do. Then the doors will open, the world will be yours, your life will be what you and I so desire! Trust Me and see."

THE TASK

July 13   Philippians 3:12; Colossians 3:23-24

"I have given you your task to do. Strain forward, therefore, with your eyes upon the goal and do what must be done. Going through the motions is not enough—that is never enough to reach a goal. Stop cheating yourself by merely going through the motions. It accomplishes little and leaves you with no satisfaction. Go forward in strength and honor, boldness and fresh enthusiasm. Go forward in My name as surely as Paul did his work in My name.

"I command you to stop holding back! Use the energy, the talents, the wisdom and the opportunities I have given to you. Use these things—do not cower before them."

THE COWARD

July 14   2 Timothy 1:7

"There is no room for cowards in My kingdom; that is why you feel so uncomfortable when you are being one. Who rules the coward? In whose kingdom does cowardice belong? Why then must it be no part of you? These are difficult questions to face up to. I ask them for your good. You must see what is at the bottom of this. Only then can you conquer the force that so desperately seeks to hold you back. Cast the chains aside, My child! Cast them totally aside in My name. The chains of fear and doubt and timidity have no business being clamped about your ankles. My children have no chains—they wear only those they borrow from Satan."

THE BOOK OF DAYS

July 15   Psalm 139:16; Colossians 1:17

"Rest in this assurance, My child. All of your days are

in My book, planned and guarded, worked out, protected. I hold all things together. Can I not hold one little life in the palm of My hand? Of course I can, especially when that life is so precious to Me.

"Every provision has been made for you, all together there in My book. Do you think I wait until the need arrives to work out My solution? What kind of forethought would that be? No, all is in place, ready to go from the moment My heart conceived you. What greater assurance could you have.? What greater security could you desire? I am your loving Father, your doting big brother, your mate and provider, your lover and friend. Could there be anything lacking, any detail unattended to, any provision unplanned for in such a loving host of providers? No, there is nothing left undone, only unrevealed. At precisely the right moment the necessary provision is presented to you. All that is required is a trusting heart, resting obediently in My care."

NEW LESSONS

July 16   John 7:38

"I have new lessons for you always, new tender words to speak to your heart. It is good to review lessons already learned, to reread messages already given, but always, always look for the new! Our relationship must be continually growing. Do not ever worry that the lessons will all be taught, the words will all be spoken, the new thoughts and ideas will all be shared. You may feel inadequate, but I am not. These words come from My Spirit, therefore they will never run out! That is what I meant by `springs of living water within you.'"

CONDUCTOR

July 17   Proverbs 4:25-27

"You have said that you need to be put back on the

right track. Consider it done. Does a train jump its track and wander about aimlessly without direction? No, it does not. It stays upon the track. It goes steadily forward, defeating all obstacles, uphill and down, straight ahead, veering neither to the right nor to the left, stopping only at the conductor's command. The train has no fear, no hesitation, no doubt of the safety or direction of its track. It leaves all that up to its master. It just keeps going, never looking back. It just keeps doing the things necessary to its route. It just keeps following the track.

"Follow Me, your Master, your Conductor, as a train follows its track. Without fear, without hesitation, without wandering where you do not belong. I will keep you on the track as you come to Me each day for instruction. Follow only the groove of obedience through the land that I take you. Yours is not to plan the route, but to follow it. So follow!"

THE GREAT PRIVILEGE

July 18   John 10:27

"Why do you not listen? Is not listening to a loved one a part of daily life? Is it not a most natural ingredient in a relationship, to simply listen? Our relationship is no different. You must not do all the talking! You must do part of the listening as well.

"I love to listen, but I also love to speak. Is it not silly to deny Me that privilege? Oh, I know, sometimes you feel that hearing Me is such a great privilege, that you do not deserve to have it unless your life is in perfect order. That is not so! If that were true, I would indeed be a silent God! Yes, to hear Me is a privilege, but I count it a greater privilege to be allowed to speak to you. So allow Me!"

THE EASY WAY

"I desire more for you. Yours is not to sit back easily and rest and wait for your life to change. No, I'm sorry, but that is not your calling. Hard work, persistence, stretching, reaching out, conquering. These things are the fabric of your life and your calling. I realize it is difficult, but I am with you. I face the challenge with you. I am here to bless each effort, to crown you with success. But only if you are willing to do what is necessary to achieve it. It is up to you, no one else. I refuse to do it for you. There would be no lesson there, no development of character. No, for your sake, I cannot work that way. You must reach out to be all that you were meant to be. It is there for you if you desire it enough to work for it.

"Life is not easy. Did I call Peter or Paul to a life of ease? Did I have a life of ease Myself? No. Why is it that you feel you deserve this easy way, that it is your right? You are capable of so much more. Would I have My talents decay within you, never being used, never being tested? Would that bring glory to God? No, I must call you to so much more. My love compels Me to do so."

UNDOUBTING TRUST

"My heart aches to have your total undoubting trust. I long to have your trust. Is there any reason why you should hold it back from Me? I long to own that precious, precious part of you that has never truly belonged to me. That part of yourself that is always held back, kept in reserve, just in case I don't come through for you, just in case I fail you. That part of you that worries and schemes and doubts and plans and will not surrender to Me."

THE REAL AND LIVING GOD

July 21   Psalm 97:10; 139:5

"Yes, you are following Me: you are My disciple as surely as the men who followed along the lakeshore and put their trust in me. We go together. My heart is thrilled to have you by My side, to share your life, to be known and loved by you! I have found friendship and love and tenderness in your presence. And what vast riches you have found in Mine!

"Together we go, undaunted, through the path of life. I live your life with you as surely as I lived My own life on earth. Every step is planned, every moment guarded; you are safe in Me. Never doubt, never fear, never feel at the mercy of anything on earth! Who or what could hope to come against Me, and you and I are one.

"The search that began in childhood has been fulfilled—you have found Me. No vision, but the real and living God!"

COME TO THE GARDEN

July 22   Matthew 26:36-39

"Heartsick and weary? Is that the condition of your soul? It need not be so, My child. Give Me your weariness, your heartaches, your doubts and fears, as I gave those things to My Father. Come to the garden as I did. Rest awhile in My presence and leave refreshed and renewed, able to handle the pressures, the heartaches of this life. Able once more to look beyond it, to look ahead to future hopes and glories. Not only to the hope of heaven—but to the hope of that next answered prayer, that next joyful gift that lies waiting for you around the bend in life's pathway! I have prepared many glad surprises, many gifts along the way! Remember that. Hang onto it when the path seems gloomy and uncertain. Let your joy bubble to the surface. I do have everything under control."

THE GREAT COMPANY

July 23   Matthew 15:19; 1 John 1:9

"Do you think yourself unworthy? You are in a great company. None of those who have done a work for Me have felt `worthy' of their calling! To feel so would be pride and a false view of one's own heart. For have I not said that the heart is desperately wicked? Why then do you find it to be so surprising? Have I not already told you the condition of the heart of man? Should it then take you by surprise to see the condition of your heart? Do you feel you must be exempt from the natural condition of man in order to be of use to Me?

"Confess your sin, yes; rout it out of your life at all costs! But do not let it stand between yourself and what I ask of you. That is the fool's way. You must follow My way. And My way is the way of humble submission, the way of obedient faith and unwavering trust. Trust in My plan for you. Trust in My ability to carry out that plan. Trust enough to see yourself as I see you. Not with a heart of pride, but with a heart of childlike wonder and belief— belief in My miracles and the working out of My will."

THE MANTLE OF PRAISE

July 24   Isaiah 61:3

"Yes, the mantle of praise! Let it cover you, envelope you, like the blanket of My love. Nestle down in its folds, let its warmth and comfort surround you at all times. Let praises spring forth, and the spirit of fainting will be replaced by the supernaturally strong and powerful Spirit of Praise!"

THE BASICS

"Back to the basics. It is always the same, always we must go back to the elementary, to the beginning, and truly begin again. Have you given everything to Me, or are you clutching dark little areas of life to your own breast? All these nagging negative thoughts and problems that keep cropping up, where are they coming from? Why have you not given them to Me? Are you not headed down the same wrong road from which I rescued you just a short time ago? The road to fear and despair.

"Look at yourself, look at these things that seek to burden you, and then tell Me—do you wish to carry them alone? Do you wish to go back to where you were before? Or do you wish to press on with Me? You must cast all of these negatives from your mind and heart. Every concern must be laid to rest, offered to Me, and left with Me. Then begin again in newness of purpose to walk with Me, to let Me carry the burdens. I will take care of these things. The spiritual, the emotional, the physical—every aspect of life is safe in Me. You are secure in My care. Had you forgotten that? Have you ceased to believe it?"

THE LOVE OF THE FATHER

"The love of the Father—that is the love I have for you. To crawl up on My lap and be encircled by My strong arms—that is your safety—that is your resting place. I am glad you have seen it at last. You are My child. You are never too old to run to this place of safety and love. The love of the Father—the cure for all ills, the strength for all trials, the answer to all questions, the solution to all problems. The love of the Father is in you!"

THE GIFT

July 27   Revelation 3:16

"Give Me your heart with no reservations, no holding back, no doubts, no doublemindedness. I cannot take your heart and fill it with Myself until you GIVE it to Me. That is all that is required. It is your gift to Me. My gift to you is to accept and fill your heart with all that I possess, with all that I am. Give Me your heart, your time, your mind, and your very being."

HALFHEARTED SEARCH

July 28   Luke 10:27

"No slipshod effort at living the Christian life will ever satisfy you. No mere dabbling in spiritual matters will ever keep you content. No halfhearted search, no lukewarm relationship with Me will ever bring happiness to you. Is your hustle and bustle, your temporal life, worth such loss? How can you possibly hope to gain more than I can give? Is the world more abundant in blessing than I, your Lord?

"Please, empty yourself that I might resume My former place. I am a jealous God. Do not steal the heart that belongs to Me, and give to any other endeavor what is Mine. It is My prized possession. Leave your heart with Me, My precious lamb. Put Me first once again. Let Me have preeminence. Let Me be your all. Let Me capture the love of your heart once more. Surrender to My love. You belong to Me."

THE CURE

July 29   1 John 4:18; 2 Corinthians 10:5

"Now that you are a child of God, you must not be a

child of fear. Perfect love casts out all fear. This fear must be cast from your life. You must decide that nothing matters as much to you as your simple obedience to me. Not even your own fears. Even your fears and feelings must be put into the background so that you can obey and serve Me.

"Concentrate upon bringing every thought into captivity to the obedience of Christ. That is, after all, where all your fear stems from—your thoughts. Bring your thought life into obedience to Me. Give to Me every single negative, fearful thought as it crops up, and let Me toss it into the sea. Let no negative thought stand between us, and the fear will have to go away. This will mean a moment-by-moment walk with Me. Literally, moment-by-moment. This is your cure. Does it seem impossible? Just trust Me one moment at a time. Take that first step and begin this close walk with Me. for this type of thing cannot be accomplished all at once. It is only accomplished each moment."

ALL WILL BE WELL

July 30   Psalm 128:1-2

"Keep believing; keep trusting. That is My word to you. One can never go wrong by trusting Me. The way may seem clouded, the answer slow in coming, but the faithful heart will look beyond and call the answer to itself. All will be well. Do I ever say otherwise? All will most assuredly be well."

THE ONLY SATISFACTION

July 31   Psalm 62:5; 32:7

"You are KNOWING Me. You are knowing Me! What a relief and a blessing that is to the heart of a God who knocks and pleads and loves and begs at the door of hearts that are deaf to My call. What pleasure I receive just from settling in beside you to enjoy your company. Yes, you have found the treasure, but I have found treasure also. The priceless treasure of a heart opened up to Me, offered to Me, belonging to Me. The treasure of earthly friendship and understanding.

"This is what it is all about. I died for this. The love of God must seek and find love in return. There is no other satisfaction. I have found this in you. You are My treasure! Enjoy My love—bask in its warmth—thrill to its touch—hide in its safety—live in its light. Be Mine forever—My love will not leave you for an instant. You have found Me. Rejoice! Rejoice as I rejoice in finding YOU!"

THERAPY

August 1   Psalm 147:3

"You need the sweet gentle therapy of God. My therapy will soothe the spirit, bind up the wounded heart, and free the tormented mind. Cling to Me if that is what you need right now. Cling to Me with all that is in you! I do not mind. I am never too busy, nor do I tire of you. Share all your hurts and fears with Me. Open your heart to Me with all its bitter disappointments and sour regrets and immobilizing fears. Let Me come in fully and wash it pure with My life-giving water, with My blood shed for you, and all your sorrows. The sorrows of today were under that blood two thousand years ago. I died for you—not just for the sins but for the sorrows as well. I died for you—now let Me live in you and through you. Let Me work in you to heal your crippled emotions, to free you from your fears. I do not judge you; I will not give up on you. We will work together on this until you can trust Me, until you can trade your fear for peace and faith. I am the great Physician."

A HEART OF LOVE

August 2   James 2:1-9

"Pride must be laid low in your character. You must be ever ready to help and aid, to comfort and lead, with no thought for self. You must see others as I see them, with a heart of love. Judge not their circumstance or character—I am the judge. My servants little qualify for this task.

"Love and help everyone. There are to be no exceptions. No one left out or thought beyond help or unworthy of it. I will choose who is to be brought into your life. If they are there, consider them to be most worthy of your endeavor on their behalf. I have brought them to you for a reason. Remember, in a guarded life there are no accidents, no chance happenings, nothing wasted. These are divine appointments—make the most of them."

ALL THINGS NEW

August 3   2 Corinthians 5:17

"More and more you will see that as I seep into your character, as My presence is allowed to flow into your life, then these character changes that you so desperately seek **will** begin to happen. My Spirit makes all things new! Not to revamp the old character but to make a new one. That is My work. Your work is to stay so close to Me, to be so absorbed in Me, that I can then do My work. The miracle work of change, of a new creation. It will be done. I have promised you that. But it will only be done as you do your part. Old attitudes, old reactions and responses, old ways of thinking and acting will be laid aside as the new creation surges forth to fill you!"

THE PLACE OF PEACE

August 4   Psalm 71:1; Proverbs 30:5; Psalm 18:2

"You have settled down into a peaceful niche with Me, your Lord. Do not leave it! This is your place of refuge and strength, no matter how the winds blow outside. You are safe here with Me. Let this contentment, this peace, this joy in My presence remain with you all the days of your life. This place of peace is your refuge here on earth and your crowning glory in the life to come. Picture it as you will—whatever your soul and the depths of your being desires—that is what I am to you. Whatever gives your heart peace and strength and power and joy—that is the place I have prepared for you. That is the place where you shall live—right here and now, in the mind and spirit, in the heart. That place is yours. I am yours! Rest here in Me. How I love you!"

A COMMON AFFLICTION

August 5   Isaiah 40:31; Matthew 11:28; Hebrews 12:2-3

"Life-weariness: a symptom common to man. No matter what the circumstance, weariness is a common affliction. Come to Me for the cure. Send others to Me for the cure! I AM the cure. I make all things new. Come to Me."

UNREASONABLE PEACE

August 6   Psalm 62:1; 119:165; Isaiah 32:17-18

"Unreasonable peace—that is what you are experiencing. Unreasonable because there seems to no earthly reason for being at peace in the situation. But yet, the peace is there. The peace is yours. It does not depend upon circumstance, it is not fed by the events in life. It is fed and maintained by the mighty Spirit of God. This is the peace I freely give to you as you spend time with Me. As you become more and more like Me. As we become one. That is the peace, the rest I promise. Your obedience brings about this peace. My promises are for the obedient heart, for the one who places absolute trust in Me. Enjoy this peace, cling to it at all costs—it is your greatest gift!"

INEXPLICABLE JOY

August 7   Psalm 126:3; 21:6

"Inexplicable joy! Another aspect of life with Me, the giver of all joy. That too is yours. It belongs to you as My child. Joy in the everyday occurrences of life, joy even when things seem to go wrong. That is the very nature of My joy, that special joy that marks My followers. Joy unspeakable and full of glory."

HEART OF GRATITUDE

August 8   Phillippians 4:6

"The heart of gratitude is one of My most priceless treasures. The heart of simple childlike thankfulness. How I respond to such a one. How I delight in doing all things well for that dear person. The one with the grateful heart!"

ALWAYS HOPE

August 9   Psalm 25:3; Proverbs 23:18

"Never lay hope aside. Whether it be hope for a material thing or hope for what you wish to become.

Always there is hope. As long as you have Me, you also have hope."

THE GREATEST OF THESE

August 10   1 Corinthians 13:13

" `The greatest of these is love.' Get love and use it at all cost! Let love be the priceless treasure of your life, that which is most earnestly sought after. A heart of love can melt any opposition, withstand any trial, soften any blow. Love does not come easily to the heart of man, but with God truly all things are possible. Take My love, unconditional and free; take it and use it lavishly upon others, upon yourself. Make My love your own."

EACH "TODAY"

August 11   Matthew 6:11; Psalm 139:16

"You have asked for My help just for today. Yes, that is the essence of My message. Just today. That is all you need help for, for surely I will be there each today of your life. You have My promise—I will not miss any of them. Look only to this day and no other. When do you lose your peace? When you look ahead, when you calculate and try to see into the days that stretch before you. Those days are Mine—this day is yours. Let Me concern Myself with what belongs to Me, and you concern yourself with what belongs to you. Is that not simple enough? Live only in today. Leave everything else to Me!"

LIVE BY FAITH

August 12   Romans 1:17

"The age-old mystery must be repeated again and

again, down through the ages, over and over to the heart of man, until it is his life—the just shall live by faith. And so I speak to you, again and again, the same sweet message, for **you** must live by faith. Giving all of your love, having all hope, all faith, no matter what the trial. Living each moment as I have taught you, no matter what. That is true faith. That is the test, the ultimate goal."

PERFECTION

August 13   Romans 15:1; Colossians 3:13; Psalm 119:96

"Must someone be perfect before you can love them? Must they fill all your needs before they are worthy of your love? What kind of test is that for frail humans to have to pass? I am the only one capable of passing the test."

THE ROAD TO TRAVEL

August 14   Psalm 119:1, 32

"You know the way—it is the way I have taught you. The way of love, totally unconditional love. The way of peace, of hope, of faith. This is the road to travel in every circumstance. When you take detours, when you go your own selfish way, then there is trouble. Then there is heartache. There is never peace on that wrong road. There is never happiness in the enemy camp. Steer clear of it at all costs!"

BRING THE NEEDS

August 15   Psalm 119:24, 35

"Do you need strength to make it one more day? Do you feel a mountain of obstacles in the way? Is your heart sore, hurting, afraid? Then you need Me. Come to Me each and every morning, no matter what the need is. No matter what the heartache, the answer is in Me. I can relieve boredom, fear, worry, pain, loss, anger, anxiety, hopelessness—all the evils of mind and spirit that plague the heart of man. But you must come to Me, you must give Me these problems. You must reach out and take the solutions. Come to Me."

TURN TO ME

August 16   Psalm 142:1-2; 141:8

"Give Me everything! Live constantly in My presence; every moment, every thought, committed to Me. Then nothing will take you by surprise, for I will be there to soften each blow. Nothing will disturb the calm within your heart. Nothing will be able to sneak in to cause heartache or fear. You need only turn to Me."

THE PATIENCE OF GOD

August 17   Psalm 57:10; 1 Timothy 1:16

"Your life would be totally Mine if only you truly understood My love and caring for you. More and more your life is Mine. I must be patient. Always I must be patient with the heart of man. I woo the heart, I shower it with love, I surround it with protection, I fill it with joy. And yet I must be patient. The heart of man is a delicate thing, slow to understand, slow to respond. It is because My love and faithfulness is so contrary to that which is learned on earth. My love, My faithfulness, must be seen and felt and understood; it must be proven over and over again. But that is all right. I am patience itself; I can wait. It is worth the wait, worth the proving, to capture and hold the hearts of My people. To love and to have their love in return. It is worth everything for that!"

THE WAY

August 18   Psalm 32:8; Isaiah 48:17

"I am showing you the way. You must not be afraid. You must not turn aside from the task I have given you to do. The task is yours, the strength is Mine. Come to Me for that strength. Come to Me for all that you need. The way is opening before you. Step through and follow the way chosen for you. It is a blessed way, a way of joy and service. The way of knowing Me."

THE BLANK PAGE

August 19   Psalm 143:8

"A blank page? Fill it with My love! A blank day? Fill it with My joy! Every morning a `blank page' stretches out before you—a page that will be filled with heartache and anger and fear, or a page that will be filled with peace and joy and love. The choice is totally yours. How do you wish the pages of your life to be written?"

LOSING CONTROL

August 20   Colossians 1:17

"Have I lost control of your life? Have I lost the power to do what must be done to hold all things together for you? Or is it you who has lost control? What does My Word say? That is the answer to your question. That is the wisdom you seek. What My Word says—that is what you must do. Anything less is not My way."

BLESSED PEACE

August 21   Colossians 3:15

"Feel My peace flood through your being. Let it well up inside you like a fountain, like a geyser! Let it burst forth from you like a river breaking free of its dam. Let My peace wash out over all those around you. Let it become the hallmark of your walk with Me for all the world to see. There is nothing so precious in life as the peace that is My gift to you. Nothing that your heart could desire, nothing that could be brought into your life through your own efforts, can compare with the wonderful, wonderful peace that I lavish upon you!"

MORE PEACE

August 22   Romans 8:6; Philippians 4:9

"You wish to know **more** of My peace? Then simply know more of Me. That is the way of peace—spending time with the Peacegiver. This gift of peace is not a gift for special occasions. It is a gift to be received every moment of your life. Seek it above all else, for only the heart resting in Me can know the joy of true contentment."

THE PATH OF PEACE

August 23   Luke 1:79; Psalm 29:11; 34:14; 37:11

"The way of peace and love and courage—more and more the path you trod. It is the path of greatest happiness, I promise you. It may not seem so at times, but truly it is. In the opposite direction lie all manner of hurt and evil. Stay on the path of peace!"

LOOK FORWARD

August 24   Hebrews 12:1

"Are you dwelling on things that are past? Are you not to look forward to run the race set before you? You cannot run a race that is behind you. That is impossible! There is no starting line. Remember, every day is a new beginning—every moment can be a new beginning."

DON'T LOOK AWAY

August 25   Deuteronomy 4:29; Psalm:34:5; 141:8

"Look at Me. Lift up your head and look at Me. Look into My eyes. See My face, behold My smile. Now, don't look away. Do you understand child? When you are looking at Me you will not be looking at the problems. You will not be rehashing old ones or creating new ones. You will not be counting up wrongs against you. You will not be dwelling on negatives or rehearsing confrontations. How could you manage to do all those things when you are looking into My face? Keep your eyes upon Me. When your focus changes, so will your attitude. It is as simple as that."

EARNING LOVE

August 26   Romans 5:8

"If I had waited to love you until you deserved it, would I ever have died for you? Would there be grace? Would I love you now? If I refused to love until man had earned My love, there would **be** no love."

BE ANGRY?

August 27   Ephesians 4:26

" `Be angry and sin not.' Let that sink in. It is all right to be angry at injustice, whether it be shown to you or to others. In fact, I was angry when on earth, was I not? But to let anger destroy you? No, that is not an answer. Whether it destroys just one precious day or a lifetime of days, that is not My will. That is why I say, `yet sin not.' You must deal with the anger you are experiencing. You must deal with it in a godly way. You must deal with the person causing it, in a gentle loving manner. Then you must give the anger to Me. There is much harm in carrying anger within you—physical, mental, emotional harm; spiritual devastation. That is why I say not to let the sun go down on your anger. You must release it to Me, not hold it inside."

FATHERLY PRIDE

August 28   2 Corinthians 7:4; Psalm 147:11

"How proud I am of you when you reach out to trust Me. When you let Me lead. When you learn a lesson I have been straining to teach you. My buttons burst with godly, fatherly pride when you obey Me."

MUCH TO GIVE

August 29   Colossians 3:23-24

"You have much to give, My child. That is why I cannot be satisfied with mediocrity in your life. That is why you must not be satisfied. A heart that is open to Me, an ear that is willing to listen, a tongue that yearns to share My voice with others. How can this be wasted? But there is much to learn, to prepare for, much to be endured before you can be fully used. Much to change in becoming one with Me."

THE PLACE OF CHOOSING

August 30   1 Corinthians 4:10; James 1:6-8

"Can you accept life as I give it to you? Are you willing to accept the challenges I place before you? Will you be a `fool' for My sake? Will you love in spite of deep disappointment and loss? Will you humble yourself, deny your rights, pick up your cross cheerfully and follow Me.? You are at the place of choosing. A double-minded man, remember him? That is what you have become. Will you give up this dual mind and bring your thoughts in line with Mine? I am asking that you do just that. You cannot serve the world and its viewpoint and serve Me at the same time. The two positions are violently opposed."

BEARING THE SORROW

August 31   Isaiah 53:3, 5

"My heart breaks for you. Do you think I am blind to your suffering? Do you think I don't understand, don't feel with you? I bear the sorrow, the deep hurting emotions, the wrenching disappointment with you. I am your constant companion. I do not only walk beside you to comfort; I live within you to feel, to hurt with you, to bear your suffering as if it were My own. It is My own, for I have made it to be so. So you see, you are not alone, you are not misunderstood, you are not on your own as you think you are. You and I are one. When you hurt I hurt—when you grieve, I grieve with you. I want you to know these things because I love you so much!"

NEVER BE AFRAID

September 1   John 10:10; 14:20

"Never be afraid, child. Don't let Satan fool you into thinking that there is anything you cannot handle. You see, it does not matter whether or not you can handle something. The question to ask is, `Can My Lord handle this?' And the answer will always be yes! There is nothing in this life that I cannot take on, and so we face things together. We do things together, we meet all the challenges of life as a team, better yet, as a force of one. We are not just two working side by side—actually we are one for I live within you. Let Me plan your days, let Me be your days. We meet this life together. Let the enemy take his fear, his discouragement, his lies, somewhere else."

TAKE OF ME

September 2   John 16:33

"Oh My child, you are taking of Me. You are reaching out and taking of Me. Appropriating Me for yourself. Letting Me be your strength, your wisdom, your love. Keep taking more! That is how to live—just keep taking more and more of Me until you are filled to overflowing. Your human frailties need not stand in your way, for you rise above them, you extend yourself by taking on My qualities and strengths. Let nothing overwhelm you. Allow nothing to overpower you. How could anything conquer the Spirit of God? And that is Who lives within you. You have all the strength and power of heaven behind you. There need be no fear ever within your heart. Hand in hand we take on the world—the Father and His dear child."

LOVE MY SHEEP

September 3   John 10:11; 21:16

"These are My sheep. You have heard about the sheep and the Shepherd. Did you know that you are a shepherd? Not the main Shepherd—that is a job only I can fill. But a shepherd just the same. This precious little flock that gathers about your table has been entrusted to you. I have placed them in your care. I have placed them in your heart forever. Love them with My love, smear healing salve all over their wounds, treasure them, lead them to Me. Always to Me, for I am the Great Shepherd and I love My sheep. I treasure them above all the wonders of earth and of heaven. My sheep are My life."

A SPOT OF HEAVEN

September 4   Psalm 127:1

"Your home is what you make it, what we make it together. It can be a place of turmoil and irritation or it can be a spot of heaven on earth. A source of strength and love or confusion and insecurity. You are the one to decide which it will be. If you will give your home to Me and follow My wise counsel, then you can guess the end result. I lead only in ways of inner peace."

TAPPED INTO THE SOURCE

September 5   James 1:5

"It is because you ask for My wisdom that I so lavishly give it. Do you know how many never ask? It is a shame upon today's world. To many I am a mere figure on a cross, a nice uninvolved friend who meets them in church on Sunday. I am not called upon for definite counsel and wisdom with which to live their daily lives. You My child, have tapped into the source of guidance and practical wisdom and knowledge simply by coming to Me. Simply by asking and seeking and then **listening** to My answer!"

GIVE IT TO ME

September 6   1 Peter 2:23; 5:6-7

"What do I always say no matter what the problem, no matter what the need? Give it to Me. That is My advice in every situation. You are not meant to handle these stresses and strains by yourself. You are not an ant that can carry many times its own weight! Man is not built that way. Give everything to Me. I know your heart, I know the situation—it must be left with Me."

SAFELY NESTLED

September 7   Psalm 37:24; John 10:28

"Yes, My dear sweet child you are safely nestled in the palm of My hand. Always see yourself there. Nothing can ever overcome you. Oh, circumstance may seem to, but only on the outside. You need never bow to circumstance on the inside. How I rejoice that you are learning that! I see the peace, the joy, the grateful heart—the acquiescence to My will, and My heart rejoices! What a lesson you have learned—what treasure you have at last taken for yourself. Never fear, I am with you. Never worry—I am at your side. Stay with Me a while—until this day is past, and then the next and then the next—just one day at a time. How I love you!"

THE SHOCK ABSORBER

September 8   Matthew 7:14

"Stay on an even keel. Use Me as your `shock absorber.' When things go wrong, when upsets come, let Me absorb the shock. Stay in perfect balance in Me. What is balance? It is the narrow way. That calm, happy heart at peace in Me. Steadiness and strength no matter how the winds blow. Joy and heart-rest, contentment and love—in the midst of every circumstance."

THE BUCKET

September 9   James 4:7; John 4:10

"It has been so long since I have spoken only because it has been so long since you have listened! I am always ready to speak, to comfort, to guide and teach the willing heart. The well does not run dry! Only, the bucket does not come down. And guess who has control over the rope? You can leave it tied above the water or you can let it down to be filled. The water does not jump into the bucket. The bucket must be lowered into the water. Do you see? Why are you trying to live this life on your own? Once again you have slipped into the snare. Depending on your own strength. Not so much deciding to do so, but just letting it happen to you. You must resist. You must wear the armor of God. Submit to Me, resist the devil and he will flee from you!"

THE CLAY

September 10   Jeremiah 18:6

"I am here—everything is all right. All is under My control. Let Me mold you. I cannot do much with a stiff neck! Clay must be soft to be molded. Be soft, be pliable, let Me show you the way. Let Me change you from the inside out. Don't resist Me. It is your `rights' or My will. One leads to joy and peace—the other to discord and pain. And it is just the opposite of what man would think. Give up your rights and cling to Me. I have so much more for you than your so called `rights' could ever give you! Trust Me."

THE WELL-WORN LESSON

September 11   Matthew 6:34

"Only today. Let that simple phrase be emblazoned upon your heart and your mind. Let it keep you where you belong—only in today. I will repeat this well-worn lesson until it is total reality in your life. Not just for a time but for always. No need to look ahead with fear and worry. No need to cast shadows upon the path before you. Life casts enough shadows without making more of them. Let the sun shine in. If you are taken care of today, then why doubt My care for tomorrow?"

THE SYMPATHETIC HEART

September 12   2 Corinthians 1:3-5; Romans 5:3;
                                              1 Peter 4:19

"Your trials and heartaches have not been just for you. They have been for others just as well. For now you have faced all manner of trials, all kinds of emotions, a myriad of circumstances. You have learned much. You have learned the hard way—now you can turn and help others. The sympathetic heart, remembering well its own bur-den, so like the burden of another, is of prime importance in My kingdom. You can understand the suffering of another, for you have suffered in like manner. And as I have held out My comfort and answers to you so too you may now turn and hold out a helping hand to those who suffer. Share with them the wisdom, the deep caring love that I have for them. Turn them away from themselves towards Me. Never regret the sufferings you endure, for they are a reservoir of treasure in My kingdom."

THESE IMMEDIATE TASKS

September 13   Psalm 116:5-6; 118:24

"Concentrate upon this moment, this day, these immediate tasks. Let all the rest go by—just simply let go of it. Not to the foggy stretches of the future, but to the warm caring hands of the God who loves you. Release all to Me. Don't hang onto a thing. No worry, no fear, no problem. Your hands should be totally empty that I might fill them."

SATAN'S ATTACK

September 14   Phillippians 4:7

"Where does Satan attack? In the mind! Remember that! That is his battleground. Resist at that point and you will win at all others. Let Me control your thoughts and he will flee. Put a firm guard over your mind and heart—I will be that guard. The power of almighty God stands sentinel over your mind. Let Me do My work!"

TO BE A SERVANT

September 15   Matthew 24:45-46; John 12:26

"I ask you to be a servant, My servant. Does the servant know what his master is doing? Must he know before he serves? Or is he a tool in the master's hand, ready and willing to serve no matter what? The servant does not pick and choose in which ways he will serve. He does not decide which service is too great. I will decide— you will serve. I know it does not make sense to you at this time, but it does not need to. You are not writing the book of life—that is My job. Misery comes when you try to be the master instead of the servant. You cannot take My place. You are only big enough to fill the place I have given you. You must learn service. We cannot move on until you have learned this lesson."

HIS BLOOD COVERS

September 16   Psalm 130:3

"Which sin did I die for? Are there any left outside, not covered by My blood? Any that you must hang onto and bear yourself, any that you must pay for yourself? Is that what My Word says or is that what Satan tells you? Don't listen to him. He is always full of lies and wants nothing but your downfall. If he cannot hurt you in one area, then he will attack in another. But he is not your master—remember that! He has no power over you. He has been defeated."

NO IDLE PROMISE

September 17   Hebrews 10:23; Psalm 145:13

"My promises are always kept. You can count on that. I do not make idle promises; I do not foster false hopes."

SUFFER THE LITTLE CHILDREN

September 18   Matthew 19:14

"Your hurts are My hurts. Your concerns are My

concerns. All that troubles you has worn its way deep into My heart—the heart of the Father. You weep with your children when they weep—you bear their pain as deeply as if it were your own—the pain of rejection. You feel it with them. I feel it too. I am here to feel, to bear, to ache, with My children big and small. Teach them to bring Me the pain as you have learned to do. Suffer the little children to come unto Me."

GLORIOUS SURPRISES

September 19   Psalm 30:5; 37:4

"Why do you stand in such amazement, My child? Did you think that all I had in store for you were trials? Oh no! I have many wonderful glorious surprises for you. Life is not all trials and it is not all joys. There is a mixture of both, necessary to flavor the `soup' of life. Of course I want to bless you. I want to fill the desires of your heart. I love to lavish gifts upon you. It should come as no surprise. Weeping may endure for a night but joy cometh in the morning. Your night was long but morning has come. Bask in the light of this new day!"

ALWAYS A REASON

September 20   Psalm 40:5

"Is it not thrilling to learn that you need never doubt Me? I will always come through for you. I will always keep My promises. When I choose the desert way you must only trust Me. There is always a reason. It is never simply chance or the fickle misfortunes of life. No, not for My children. There is always a reason, always a plan."

THE HAND OF PEACE

September 21   John 8:44; 1 John 4:18

"Never doubt, for I am not the one to lay the cold hand of fear upon your heart. That is never My work. It is the work of the liar himself. Peace, My child. I lay the hand of peace upon you. Never the hand of fear, but always of comfort and peace. All is well. How many times I have said it and I say it now. All is most assuredly well! He is the father of lies. Say it over and over again—read it like a banner burned across the sky."

THE TIME TO PLANT

September 22   Matthew 13:23

"Yes, sit at My feet and learn from Me. The ground is worked up. It is rich and fertile and accepting of good seed. Now is the time to plant—to plant My way of doing things. My way of living your life. I give the seed liberally and gladly. Take My seed; sprinkle it happily throughout the furrows of life. We plant a garden of great peace, of great beauty. A garden of love. A garden of delights."

DAUGHTER OF THE KING

September 23   Revelation 17:14

"A frightened child? The child of the King frightened? It need never be so. Who would dare to harm the child of the King? I will reassure you over and over again as many times as is it necessary, that all is well. You are in My hand. Let Satan huff and puff—he cannot blow the house down! You are safe inside with Me."

STEP BY STEP

September 24   2 Corinthians 11:3; Romans 8:12-13

"Life with Me is so simple. Remember, the simplicity of Christ. Just one step at a time, simply, easily through life we go. A situation arises—come to Me—how would I have you handle it? Then do as I have taught you. Do not react in the flesh; react in the Spirit. Do not trust your own counsel—seek Mine. Do not believe or even listen to the lies of Satan. Come to Me for truth. Let My Spirit, My very being, totally fill and engulf you. This is the way to live. Not struggling in darkness, not languishing in emptiness, not straining against the yoke. But simply, easily, joyfully, in My power—step by step through life with Me."

TREMENDOUS LOVE

September 25   John 6:39

"How I love you! How I lavish My love upon you in great generous helpings! The love of God is boundless, unequaled, in all the universe. None can slip from My grasp, none can go beyond My love, for there are no limits, no conditions to the tremendous love of God. Rest easy in this love. Curl up and rest easy each and every moment of your life. I am with you, I am beside you, I am within you. I am the great `I AM.' Never do you walk alone, never do you work alone, never do you breathe a breath without Me, without My watchful love surrounding you, cushioning you from all of life's blows."

THE NAME

September 26   Hebrews 12:1; Romans 8:15

"Never seek to handle life in your own small strength, not even for a moment. How Satan loves to sneak in in such moments and capture you. He binds you in chains of fear and doubt and timidity. Worry, anxiety, spilling over from the depths of hell into the hearts of My people. It must not be allowed. He has no rights over you. I will keep him at bay if you will let Me. The mere sounding of My name carries great power over the demons of hell. You are safe in Me."

NO OTHER JUDGE

September 27   Colossians 2:16

"You must do what you know to be right in every situation. No one else can judge for you. No one, no matter how dear they may be to you, can judge or direct your life. They do not understand. You must accept this and rely upon Me—for My guidance, for My perfect understanding. Do not let their misguided judgment or advice wound you. They mean you no harm. They simply have not the means to understand or judge rightly. Give Me the pain, the misunderstanding—let Me bear it. It need not be a burden to you. It need not be a wound. Give Me this pain, My child. Give it totally to Me."

NO UNFORESEEN DETOURS

September 28   1 John 5:18

"Nothing can harm you, child. Therefore, there is nothing to fear, nothing to dread. Nothing to get upset about. You will find more and more as we travel life's roads together, that there are no unforeseen detours. I am your guide. I am your protector!"

BECOMING ONE

September 29   1 John 5:20

"How dear you are to Me. How I love to hold you in

My heart, to be your all. How I love our time together. The closer you get to Me, the more we actually become one. One in the Spirit, one in mind, one in all ways, human and divine."

PEACE ON THE THRONE

September 30   Isaiah 26:3; Philippians 4:7

"Let My peace reign. Let it be king, total controller of your life. Put peace on the throne, not worry or fear or nervousness. Let peace have its way in your life. I am that peace. It is not a gift to be sought after, it is simply Me. Let Me control you and peace will abound. It will flourish in the life lived close to Me."

NO SAFER PLACE

October 1   Psalm 146:5-9

"You must entrust all things into My care. Not just for yourself but for others also. Take the things that you desire so much for others and place them in My hands just as you place your own needs and desires with Me. Because you give them to Me, I care for them just as I care for your needs. There is no safer place for your concerns."

OUR PATH

October 2   Psalm 119:32

"You are learning the way of trust and hope. Learning how to walk life's paths with Me. Each new lesson, added one upon another, forms the narrow path beneath your feet. It is a narrow way, but not a dangerous way, for I walk it with you. There is no danger, there is no chance, there is no reason ever for fear! It is OUR path, yours and Mine, designed specifically for our feet."

GIFTS FROM THE HAND OF GOD

October 3   James 1:17

"Consider all to be My gifts. Your life, its joys, its challenges—all I have given. All gifts from the hand of God. Gifts for your pleasure, for your joy, for your learning and growing—for refreshment and love, for peace and safety. All are treasures from the God who loves you! My provision in all of life is My testimony to My great love and care for you and yours."

THANKFULNESS

October 4   Colossians 2:7

"Yes, be grateful. Be very very thankful! This thankfulness and the trust that produces it, opens the storehouse of God. It is My pleasure to serve you, to bless you with all good things. Your thankfulness is your seal of approval upon My glad gifts to you!"

LIFE'S GREATEST JOY

October 5   2 Timothy 2:21

"To be used by Me—life's greatest joy. To feel and know—to be in the very center of God's `working out,' His precious plan! Not only My plan for you, but My plan for others as well. Think what joy I experience in this process—what joy I know when My children USE Me. Stay close to Me. Many opportunities will come. Many dear hurting children of Mine will be brought to you.

Accept them all—love them with My love—share all that I am, all that you know Me to be, simply and openly with them. I will heal—I will bless. I will draw them to Myself. You will be My stepping stone."

LOOK TO THE GOOD

October 6   Philippians 4:8

"Look only to the good. Look only to what you have, to what God has given you. Do not let your eyes come to rest upon any other thing but the blessings and peace of Christ. Do not fix your gaze upon the negatives, upon the past or the future. Remember, your life is hid with Me. By now you know that I can be trusted and that I have all your affairs in My hands. Not one thing escapes My attention."

SIMPLE TASKS

October 7   Psalm 37:4; 119:47

"Accept your tasks with joy and with the energy and strength that I so abundantly lay upon you. Meet all of life with gladness to be doing My will. Simple though it be, every task done according to My desire carries special blessings. Submit to Me in bubbling unending joy and learn to delight yourself in Me and in My will for you. Delight yourself in the simple tasks I have appointed to you this day."

HEART OF LOVE

October 8   1 Corinthians 13:13

"The heart of love! How I see that in you! Pure, wonderful childlike love for your God. What a joy it is when so many disregard, when so many hate Me. Your love is healing balm to the wounds of the Father. I find great joy in answering your prayers. The grateful happy heart is a wondrous treasure to Me. Let your love shine through, out to a hurting world that does not know or trust Me."

HEALING TOUCH

October 9   Isaiah 53:5

"I am the healing balm for all of life's wounds, all of its pains and sorrows. You have only to come to Me. Sup with Me, share with Me—open up the hurting recesses of your heart in My presence. The mere exposure to My light is healing enough. There is no sorrow on earth too great for My healing touch. You are My precious child, one I hold so dear, so near to My heart. Bring Me your griefs and sorrows, your hurts and pains, your tears and heartaches. Share them with Me. Then take My peace, My healing, and comfort back again with you."

SPIRITUAL ENERGY

October 10   Psalm 29:11; Isaiah 40:31

"How can you have the necessary strength to help others? You know the answer. That strength, that wisdom, that spiritual energy can only come from its source. Come to the Source to receive all you need to bless and help others. Stop several times each day to draw upon My strength if need be. Immerse yourself in My Spirit. Then you will have the emotional vitality to carry on, to do all that I have called you to do. The task is great, but My power is greater still."

THE MOUNTAIN MOVER

October 11   Matthew 17:20

"Do not feel as though you have come to a mountain that must be moved! I am the Mountain Mover! Just follow Me, follow My instructions one step at a time. That is all I ever ask of you. Never more than that. Do what must be done each day, seek My guidance for the rest, and leave all of it in My hands. You are not responsible for the outcome. You are only responsible for the part I ask you to play. Bring the burdens of others to Me, lead the burdened seeking souls to My doorstep. I will care for them as surely as I care for you. Just bring them to Me."

THE TRAP

October 12   Romans 8:31-37

"What could be overwhelming this moment? Are you not overwhelmed when you are looking ahead, counting all the moments together instead of one at a time? And how must these moments be lived, My child? All at once or just one at a time? Again you have fallen into Satan's trap. He loves for you to see mountains, to think things insurmountable, to view all that you must do as one great unconquerable force. But that is not reality in My kingdom. My reality is one task performed in My power, one moment, one step at a time. Then on to the next and the next. Put your priorities in order and go through them with the strength of Christ."

SECURITY

October 13   Psalm 112:8; Proverbs 14:26

"I am your security! Could you want anything more than the God of all the universe as security? My name, My

Spirit, My pledge to you, the promises of My Word—
these are your security, your fortress, your salvation.
Why think upon any thoughts of insecurity? It makes no
sense. Rest yourself in Me. Think upon the pure, the
lovely, all that is good. There is not one single thing in
your life now or in your future life that I cannot handle. So
why worry and fret about it?"

READY ANSWER

October 14   Psalm 55:22

" `The Lord will take care of that.' That is to be your
ready answer to every problem life presents. Simply—
`The Lord will take care of that.' Then on your way, My
child, simply on your way!"

MIGHTY WIND

October 15   Isaiah 59:19

"Power over Satan belongs to you in My name as My
child! He has been conquered, but so few believe it. Know
and believe that his power is as straw before the mighty
wind of God's power! Rebuke him, chastise him, bind
him in chains. He has got to flee. You have learned a secret
of victorious living."

RELAX

October 16   Psalm 46:10

"Relax in Me. This is all you need. To be with Me. No
matter what cares threaten, come to Me, spend time with
Me, feel the cares that press so deeply just melt away in
My presence."

I AM DADDY

October 17   Romans 8:15-16

"Never feel overwhelmed. You are small but I am big! You are weak but I am strong. The strength of a `Daddy,' a dear loving Daddy, is yours, My child. Yes, I am not just Father—I am Daddy. People don't understand this because they have not the child-heart that I long for them to have. But My people, great and small, young and old— they all need a daddy to run to. A lap to climb onto, a shoulder to cry on, a chest to burrow into. Is this not the only comfort, the only answer when life gets tough? Just hide yourself in Me."

THE CHILD-HEART

October 18   Luke 10:21; 1 John 3:1

"Oh, the secrets of the child-heart! The precious heart of the child. No matter the age, no matter the circumstance—you are My child, My precious blood-bought child. Man is so busy being `man' that he misses My calling. The calling to be `child.' Bring Me the bumps and bruises, the hurts great and small. Bring Me the questions, the concerns, all the `dailyness' of your little day. Bring it all to Me—keep nothing back to brood over—bring it all to Me. I will take care of everything."

A TOUCH FROM GOD

October 19   Isaiah 40:11

"A touch from God, is that your desire? Then you have only to come to Me. Can I touch one who does not come close? Come close to Me and you will receive your touch from God!"

THE WAY OUT

October 20   2 Corinthians 12:10; Psalm 40:17

"You know that difficult days must come. But they can be lived through with My strength. I am so proud of you, for you are learning this. You are living it at last. My heart rejoices to see your calm trust, your willing obedience, your change of heart. How I treasure you and all that you have learned! Stay steady—do not falter—do not succumb to Satan's taunts and pestering. Keep the foot of faith planted firmly upon his head and all will be well. I will show you the way out of many difficulties—you have only to follow Me."

ABSORB

October 21   Luke 10:39, 42

"This has been a time of absorbing My will, My outlook, My plan in your life. Absorbing Me. Let it always be so! Continue on in quiet blessed absorption, in peaceful loving friendship with Me. Continue to gaze upon Me in wistful love and adoration—never trade this child-love for cold sterile formulas, for going through the motions. Cuddle up in Me; look upon My face; let My warmth and love settle into your being. Depend upon this for your nourishment, for your very life. Look to Me in gentle wonder for all things. I am everything to you! I am all you could need or desire. There is nothing more—there is no better. Absorb!"

THE BEGINNING

October 22   Psalm 141:1-2; 139:18

"Is it so difficult to be mindful of this one thing? To

meet with Me at the beginning of each new day. All else will follow. All else will spring from this joyful sharing-time. All of life will fall into place if the day is begun in this way."

BUSY DAYS

October 23   Ephesians 6:11

"There is always time enough to meet with Me. Do you fail to brush your teeth, to comb your hair, to eat on busy days? Am I so unimportant then? Let the busy days come—but face them in My strength, in My armor—come to Me for that each morning and all will be well."

DENYING ME

October 24   Titus 1:16

"Shall you deny the power of God in your life? That is what you are doing when you refuse to come to Me. You are not just neglecting Me, as you so often think. No, you are denying Me. To whom much is given, much will be required. You must use the power of God that is meant for you. To fail in this is to fail in all of the important things."

NO MIDDLE GROUND

October 25   Revelations 2:4

"Do not fail Me. I did not call you to failure, to disregard, to denial, and disobedience. Who is the one who calls you to such as these? Surely not the Spirit of God! Who then is winning? Who is wooing you away from Me? Oh, I know, your heart stands fast. But what of your mind, your time, your purpose? What of these? You must return to Me in every way. There is no middle ground. There can be no compromise. Have you talked yourself into believing such folly? I must have you wholly and completely. There is no other way. Anything less is as nothing at all. Remember, it is you who have chosen—you chose to follow Me at all costs, in all ways, for all time. I did not force those words from your lips. You spoke them of your own accord. Am I now to settle for less than your promise? No, My child, I accept what is given to Me. Do not try to take back what is Mine. I shall not be satisfied with anything less than all you are, all you have, all you are to become. I have paid the price. You are Mine!"

THE ROOT OF GOOD

October 26   Matthew 19:17; James 1:17

"The root of all good—that is God. All good comes from Me. Do you wish to see good in your life? Do you wish to do good, to be good? Then come to the source where all good is supplied. Only there will you find your heart's desire."

WORDS OF HOPE

October 27   Romans 8:25; 15:13

"Do you seek words of hope? You need only look to Me, to My Word! All of life is hope when lived in Me, for I am hope itself. There need be no resignation to failure or defeat when I am in the picture! I am life and power and hope, and I give these things to you. Do not allow anyone or anything to steal your hope, for I have given it to you Myself!"

REACH OUT

October 28   Matthew 10:39

"Do not allow yourself to get so wrapped up in self. Instead, let yourself be wrapped up in Me, in the people around you. You will find happiness there, in your experience of Me, in your involvement with others. It is a rich world for those who seek to reach out beyond the bounds of their own existence. It is a world filled with wonder, filled with the splendor of sharing and reaping! Reach out to others, give of your time, your talents, your riches. Reach up and reach out and your life will be filled with treasure. Reach out in My name and be free."

NO LACK

October 29   Psalm 34:9

"Never let yourself feel any lack, for with Me there is none. I fill all in all. You may not as yet feel or see the answer, the fulfillment of your need, but it is there, waiting to be revealed. Waiting to be discovered by the faithful heart. Do not think `There is not enough!' Instead, think only `The Lord will supply!' Then watch in wonder as My plan is revealed. Go along in quiet confidence, waiting for the need to be met."

THE GROOVE OF OBEDIENCE

October 30   Psalm 143:10; Galatians 5:25

"Let the Spirit direct you. When you know in your heart, in your spirit, which way to go—when it seems clearer and more sure each time you come into My presence, when all other options seem outside the groove of obedience, then follow. It is an awareness, a simple quiet confidence that saturates your mind and heart as you trust in Me. The way is made clear as you go."

MY MESSAGE

October 31   Ephesians 1:23

"I am Protector, Master, Teacher, Friend—I am all to you. I do all for you. Whatever role you need Me to fill— I am. This above all is My message to you. My message of comfort and light."

WONDER GIFTS

November 1   Psalm 103:2-5; 145:19

"Little treasures of the Kingdom. Have I not promised these things? How gladly I prepare them for you. How My heart sings at the thought of your happiness in My supply! I treasure these moments with you—the glad surprise, the joy of answered prayer, the wonder of seeing My hand in all things. I prepare these wonder-gifts for you much as you prepare gifts for your children. With a heart of love, with a tender hand, with joyful expectation! Your obedience releases My hand of blessing."

THE ANSWERS

November 2   Proverbs 2:6; Colossians 2:3

"The wisdom that you need for any task is found in Me. No need to look and search and struggle for the answer—just come to Me. I have the wisdom—I have the answers—come to Me and I will share them."

EARTHLY THINGS

November 3   Luke 14:33

"You must be willing to surrender your richest treasures to Me. The things that mean the most to you. Not so that I can take them away, but so that I can hand them back to you with My blessing. Do not let these earthly things come between us. Are they worth that?"

LET GO

November 4   Psalm 46:10

"Release yourself to Me. Just let go. You are always holding back. Just relax and let go!"

THE SECRET OF SURRENDER

November 5   Hebrews 6:1

"Total surrender—that is what I ask of you. Why do My messages speak to the same problems time and time again? Because the lesson has not been learned, that part of you has not yet been surrendered. Always there are new things to learn, but first the old lessons, the elementary things must become a part of you. We cannot move on before you are ready. Just let go, My little one. That is all; that is the secret of surrender. Not to the unknown, not to a void, but to Me the trusted Friend, the gentle Saviour, the One who holds all things together. When you let go and let Me take over, then the miracles begin."

NO LACK

November 6   Psalm 23:1

" `The Lord is my shepherd; I shall lack nothing!' This

is to be your verse for all days to come. Remember it always. Hide it close to your heart. Its wonder shall be fulfilled. Have you not seen the miracles I work for My faithful children? It is My joy to work them for you. Lean on Me—there is no lack. Help comes from places you would not dream of looking. Guidance and counsel is yours in abundant measure. It is My joy to serve you—it is My desire, My pleasure. I am your shepherd—you shall lack nothing!"

NO MERE ACCIDENTS

November 7   Luke 15:20

"I know all. I am prepared for all things. Nothing slips past Me unnoticed. No mere accidents happen to My children. Nothing is unplanned for, nothing left to chance. Rest in this. Relax in My wonderful care for you. Slip into My strong arms like a tired child and rest there, trusting Me. All is well. All is well."

NARROW VISION

November 8   1 John 3:16; 4:7

"Look at others through the eyes of love—My love. Do this for Me! What does it accomplish to see them in your own narrow vision? Are their lives made better? Are you enriched? Are they changed into My image, or are you? No. Nothing positive ever comes from viewing others in the natural vision of the heart of man. Only as you see them with My eyes of love do they blossom into that which I see them to be. Trust Me enough to do this favor for Me. Look at all you meet with My love and respond to them with that love. Miracles will happen when you trust Me enough to do this."

PRAYER IS REAL

November 9   James 5:16

"A new way of looking at things—that is what you need and that is what the prayers of My people are giving to you. A new insight into life, a new viewpoint, a clean fresh way of seeing the circumstances of life. From this fresh outlook springs joy and peace and hope eternal. Never feel that the prayers of others are futile. Always they enrich life, they change things, they lift you up on wings of strength. Can you not feel the prayers of My people on your behalf? In My kingdom, prayer is not just words! Prayer is real. It can be seen and felt and known. Never fail to ask for prayer and never fail to pray for others."

IN HIS STRENGTH

November 10   Philippians 4:13

" `I can do all things through Him who strengthens me.' This does not mean that you can somehow, in a mediocre way, manage to muddle through all things in My strength. No, that is not the idea. Doing all things in My strength is to do them with calm, joyful, peaceful strength. Willingly, obediently, lovingly doing all that I ask you to do. This can be done. It can be done by YOU. With your personality, with your particular problems, with every circumstance of your life—it can still be done. You must believe this. You must begin to live it. It is not a fairy tale nor a future plan or hope—this type of life is what I call you to NOW, this very moment."

A NEW CHOICE

November 11   Galatians 5:16-17

"Each day a new choice must be made—to live in Me

or to live in self. One must always be set aside for the other, for they cannot co-exist. There need be no muddied view. It is crystal clear—you live for Me or you life for self. How will you live this day?"

THE LISTENING EAR

November 12   Ephesians 6:11; John 10:27

"Keep the listening ear tender and watchful so you do not miss the way. Satan will do his best to distract you, to keep you from My purpose. Do not let him succeed. Turn to Me daily, moment by precious moment. Ponder the things of God, respond to My great love, be ever vigilant, ever aware of My presence and My plan unfolding for you. Do not let yourself become sidetracked, but stay on the narrow way of obedience. Walk it with Me in awesome splendor—the quiet splendor of two hearts joined as one!"

FREE INDEED

November 13   Galatians 5:1

"Yes indeed—free you are free and free you shall be. No child of Mine must be slave to anything—not the things of the world and not the lies of Satan. Let him grumble and moan and roar in anger—he cannot harm you. Keep him constantly in My light and he must go cowardly away. He is angered—it matters not. His hold is broken. Stay with Me here, lifted up above his tricks and torments. Learn to recognize him every time he rears his head and keep him in his place! I am Lord!"

THE TRUE LIFE

November 14   Ephesians 5:8-10

"Living with Me, that is what true life is. Opening up

each area of your life to Me and letting Me come in to fill you with My glorious presence. What life can possibly be gloomy or sad or boring when it is lived in My presence? Surrender to Me, let down all barriers, remove all obstacles—let Me fill every nook of your existence. I turn mere existence into LIFE!"

THE PLACE OF POWER

November 15   Acts 1:8

" `Ye shall have power...' More and more you shall learn what is meant by this. You have come to the place of power by following the narrow path of faith and obedience. And power you shall have! One cannot live in close union with Me without experiencing My godly power."

NEW LEVELS

November 16   Numbers 14:8; Psalm 61:2

"Do not be afraid! Do not hold back. Do not keep Me at arm's length. The new lessons I have for you are not frightening. You are ready for them—they will not harm you. Trust Me! Reach out your hand to Me and let Me lead you onto new levels of experience in Me. I take you slowly, step by step. You are going now beyond the present limits of your understanding, but could you have a more sure guide to lead you? Are you afraid to venture forth past familiar landmarks? I know where I am going and I hold your hand. Just let Me take you. Surrender totally to Me."

SUPERNATURAL CONTENTMENT

November 17   Psalm 132:5

" `A place for the Lord!' Yes, there must always be a

place for the Lord if you are to be happy and content. Contentment follows peace with Me. It cannot come of its own accord—it comes with Me! It is a part of Me. If you resist or neglect Me, you forfeit the contentment that is a by-product of meeting with Me. This is supernatural contentment, godly peace. Allow yourself this peace, this utter contentment in Me."

THE PUZZLE

November 18   Proverbs 4:18; 8:14

"Life is a puzzle—I fit the pieces together so perfectly. Why struggle so with clumsy, child-like hands when I know exactly where all the pieces go? Once again let Me put life in its proper order, each piece in its perfect place. Let Me balance all the wonderful facets of your life in perfect harmony, resulting in utter child-like contentment."

ONLY FOLLOW

November 19   John 21:21-22

"You must not judge your life by the standards of this world. Your life is not to be lived according to the world's plan, but according to Mine. Do not let worldly criticism wound your heart. It is not their place to question you or offer earthly advice or admonition. They do not understand the choices I have made for you. It is not their place to understand or approve or disapprove. Take courage— do not give them the opportunity to pity you. Show forth the strength of the Lord in your life—show forth My joy! In the end they will see and they will be amazed at My providence, at the culmination of My plan for you. Follow Me where no one else would follow. I am calling you to the pathways of your life—I am not calling them. Dare to keep following in spite of worldly opinion. Seek only to follow, to walk in My footsteps, to be free!"

BARRIERS

November 20   Psalm 18:29

"I tear the barriers down with My light—the barriers that you build about yourself through self-pity, fear, and disobedience. They are torn down—do not rebuild them. The barriers not only keep others out, but they also keep you from entering in to joy and peace and love. These walls you throw up for your `protection' are really devices of Satan to keep you defeated. When you feel a barrier rising up about you, come to Me for its demolition!"

BE VULNERABLE

November 21   John 12:24

"Be vulnerable. That is what I ask of you. I know it is difficult; it seems risky, but truly it is safe. It is the way of happiness in Me. Be vulnerable in My strength when your own fails. You are safe in Me."

NO LOOKING BACK

November 22   Luke 9:62

"When you knelt before Me years ago and declared your desire to follow Me—that was the day I put My plan into action. That day you gave Me permission to work out My best for your life. Do not look back now. Be fit for My service; be strong in the waiting; be courageous in mind and loving in heart. Do not block My way through rebellion and anger and worldly viewpoint. Stand against the lies of Satan, against the current of the world, against the ravages of earthly thought. Stand and stay standing! Bow down before Me, seek only My will, hang on to the end. You will look back with joy!"

GENTLE UNDERSTANDING

November 23   Psalm 147:5

"People do not understand—they cannot always understand. Do not expect it. You will only receive true understanding from Me. When you truly come to realize this, you will not be so disappointed in others. That is why man needs Me, for the constant gentle understanding that only I can give."

SURRENDER IS THE KEY

November 24   Romans 12:1

"Surrender. That is the key to quality of living in Me. At last you have surrendered in sureness of purpose to My will for you. Do not be afraid—the hallmark of My surrendered child is lack of fear. Waver not upon the sea of doubt. Stand firm and true, courageous and unyielding, for all the world to see."

HEAVENLY TREASURE

November 25   Ephesians 3:19

"Yes, you are learning! As you let go of the things you are grasping in tight little fists, I am free to fill those open hands with My choicest blessings. It is a law of My kingdom that I cannot fill what is already full! If your hands and heart are full of earthly treasure there is no room for heavenly treasure. It must be one or the other that fills you. As you let go of self, of your limited ideas of how things should be, then I am free to give you Myself, My attitudes of Joy and service, My plans for your life. Keep letting go!"

AVAIL YOURSELF

November 26   Mark 6:50; 1 Corinthians 16:13

"Rely more and more upon My wise counsel. It is here for you, waiting to be called upon, to be used. Avail yourself also of My courage. It takes raw unswerving courage to do the things that are necessary to succeed. It is not an easy challenge that you face. It is an unending struggle to reach out beyond yourself, to reach higher and further than the time before. It takes strength and courage that you will find in Me. Claim it for yourself to assist you in your task."

PREPARATION

November 27   Ephesians 2:10; 2 Timothy 2:21

"All these things are for a reason. You are not lead down varied paths for no specific reason. Each step leads to another, each task is a preparation. You wish to serve Me—that service must go according to My plan, My best plan! There must be a time of preparation before each upward step."

CHOICEST BLESSINGS

November 28   Galatians 5:1

"I wish also to serve you! To do so is My joy and

desire. Allow Me to serve you with the choicest blessings of My kingdom: genuine strength, inimitable courage, divine wisdom, supernatural grace, godly love. These are the riches I extend to you. Hide them in your heart and be free. Free from tension, free from strife, free from fear and anger and all negative debilitating influences! Free to be joyful and full of peace, lighthearted and carefree. Reach out for your heart's desire!"

DEVOTION

November 29   Ezekiel 34:26

"You covet My blessing, My blessing you shall have! I hold nothing back from a heart of love, a heart filled with devotion to Me. Just go along the simple path I have shown you. The calm quiet path of peaceful, joyful obedience, of hard work, of trust in Me. My hand of blessing is upon you. Live your life as I have taught you and all will be well as I have planned it."

LIFETIMES OF THOUGHT

November 30   John 8:47

"Just give Me opportunity and wait in expectant silence, and I gladly speak. I have much to say. Therefore, do not limit Me to your human expectations. I do not run out of words. I have lifetimes of thought to share with you. Lifetimes of love. Test Me and see—My abundance extends to all things, even My words to you. Do not cheat yourself. Do not let Satan steal from us."

THE GOD OF ANSWERS

December 1   John 4:13-14

"Is there a need I cannot fill? No, there is not. Is there

a heartbreak I cannot heal? No, there is not. Is there a vainly searching heart I cannot satisfy? No, there is not. Is there a storm I cannot still? By now, you know the answer. Share the answer with others. Do not merely listen to their problem, to their heartache, and nod and offer understanding. That is not enough. You are in a position to offer so much more. You are offering sand, when you could be giving springs of living water. Open up to these suffering ones. Lay yourself open before them. Let them truly see the God of strength and peace, the God of answers."

LIKE SMALL COINS

December 2   Colossians 2:6; 3:2

"How many days have been spent like small coins slipping through the fingers of one who has many? How many days have been spent in your own pursuits, in your own power? The things you are doing are not bad, they are not wrong, nor are they against My will for you. No, they are good things—but must you do them alone? May I not share in them? May I not be intimately involved in your days, in your work? Why am I left behind? Am I not your friend, your Lord? Spend your days with Me. You will see the blessing for doing so."

THE BREAKFAST BELL

December 3   John 15:9; 17:23

"Yes, My child, strength for all the tasks and trials of life—that is My provision, My gift to you each brand new day. Come and get it! I cannot ring a breakfast bell each day, but I do call you to the table of My delights each and every morning. You are a most welcome guest—not only a guest, a child as well. What father would not miss the face of his daughter at the breakfast table? What father would not be hurt to see his child scurry off to meet the day without a word of love to send her on her way—without a touch, a smile, a warm breakfast to sustain her? Do you see the `humanness' of God, of My fatherhood in this? The love of the Father is always with you. Come and get it!"

CHOICES

December 4   Job 13:15; Matthew 26:39

"The gentle way of trust and obedience, the simple child-heart, is so very precious in this world of demands and manipulation. How much better to leave the choices to Me, to trust completely in My care of you, rather than to make demands based on human viewpoint. I love you too much to instantly gratify your every desire in a way that truly is not best for you. All of life must work together, not just the part you see. This is why a trusting heart is so vital to My plan. The next time that you are tempted to demand from your Lord, stop, turn to Me in childlike wonder and simply leave the matter in My hands."

YOUR SONG

December 5   Psalm 29:11; 73:26

"The strength of the Lord will see you through! That is to be your song, the song and the banner of your heart. What could you ever face that I cannot see you through? There is nothing in heaven or on earth. Always My strength is with you. Though your own may fail you, Mine never will. And it is yours in abundant measure!"

TAKE ALL

December 6   John 1:16; 10:10

"Never do I hand out My gifts in meager portions. It is only man who takes the meager portion and leaves the abundance lay behind, unused, unclaimed. Let it not be so in your life. Take all that I have for you. All the strength, all the love—unconditional, godly love from the heart divine. It is yours—take and use. Lavish it upon all those in your life. It is free and abundant from the hand of God. Take all the wisdom, all the peace, all of everything that I am and give to you. Leave nothing behind. Do not be satisfied for one moment to go away empty-handed or lack anything from the throne of grace. It all belongs to you, My child. Take and use."

ONLY SPEAK

December 7   1 John 5:14

"The power of the ages is at your disposal. Only speak and it shall be so! Only ask and it shall be given. That is the gift, the right of the soul linked so closely to Mine. For that soul shall not ask amiss. That soul, so close to Me in thought and spirit, shall know and claim the will of God. And it shall be done!"

CONSUMING LOVE

December 8   1 Peter 4:8

"Have a heart of love, My love. More and more let this love consume you. This is the only love that can possibly wash over all the difficulties of life, all the hurts and pain caused by man toward one another. Only this love can cover a multitude of sins. Seek actively to have this love more a part of your life. What is gained by hatred, by all the negatives that surface from this lack of love? Nothing is ever gained in this way. Nothing."

A TOUCHABLE GOD

December 9   Psalm 24:3-4

"Touching the heart of God—this is not something to be reserved for special occasions. You may always touch the heart of the God who loves you and longs to be touched, to be understood, to be used. If there is one thing I am not—it is aloof. My children may see Me as such and so hold Me off at a distance, but it is not I who holds back. I am always willing and ready to flood My children with My presence. I am always touchable. One need only come to Me with a clean heart, made clean by My own sacrifice. A clean, open heart is all that I require. A clean heart and a listening ear. A spirit willing to be lead, to be molded. These are the things most precious to a touchable God."

THE POTTER

December 10   Isaiah 64:8

"Give Me this day. Make yourself pliable in My hands. I am the Potter and I do all things well. As My power flows through you, as you listen and obey My directions, then you also will do all things well. One who truly follows My Spirit does what is best because My Spirit guides in no other direction."

THE GUIDE

December 11   1 Chronicles 28:9

"Is guidance your heart's desire? It is a noble desire,

My child. To be guided one must spend abundant time with the Guide. Does one cast off on unfamiliar waters alone, expecting the guide to then swim out from shore to instruct and give the necessary guidance? Hardly anyone today takes the Guide along. Let Me get in the boat. You get so busy, so `efficient,' so wrapped up in life, that you sometimes leave Me on shore. Then in confusion and frustration, you look about yourself and say, `Now where is the guidance? Why does it not come?' Yet the Guide is waiting patiently back on shore. If I am to be your guide, I must be alongside you there in the boat of life. A casual relationship will never do. Have I not said that when you seek Me with all your heart, that I shall be found by you?'"

CALM DOWN

December 12   Psalm 107:29-30

"Calm d-o-w-n. Calm down in your spirit, in your mind, in your body. Let My peace and tranquility flow through you. You have been very busy, very involved. I understand. But now it is necessary to calm yourself and be filled with My quiet. Time to take a deep breath and do one thing at a time in My strength and peace. Carry this peace, this serenity, with you throughout the day. Come to Me for it each morning and then continue on in My peaceful presence all day long. This is the way to truly live."

ALL IS REWARDED

December 13   Psalm 19:11; Ephesians 6:8

"I love you. That is what I wish to say to you today. I love you, with all of your inconsistencies, your weaknesses, and muddled confusion. You see those things—I see only a heart of love, a precious child, one after My own heart. You see the failures; I see the victories, and each one is added to your account. So small in your eyes that you may fail to see them, but nothing escapes the eyes of God. All is recorded—all is rewarded. Let My love wash over you, settle you down, lift you up and carry you through. Say it often—`God loves me.' "

DO THINGS RIGHT

December 14   1 John 3:7

"Do things right. This is the law of My kingdom. If you do each thing in your life the right way; if you obey My laws and trust in Me for the result, if you surrender all of life to Me, and humbly submit to My way of doing things in every situation, then your life will be right. It cannot be wrong. This is the lesson I have been speaking to your heart, `Do it My way!' Blessings above and beyond all you could desire—that is the reward, the result of obedience."

THE WAY OF THE KINGDOM

December 15   Isaiah 58:11

"Faith steps in when fear takes over. Simply allow your faith in Me, in My promises, to guide you, to oust the fear that tries to hold you back from obeying Me each step of the way. Follow then the way of the Kingdom. Doggedly follow each step of the way. There is a path—follow the Master—it is the right road to all of your heart's desires."

SUCH AS YOU

December 16   John 15:16

" `What can I say to someone such as you?' you ask. My child, you do not need perfect ears to hear Me. You do not need a virgin heart to love Me. I need one `such as you,' for there are no others any **different**. I need only open hearts and listening ears. There is no perfection on the face of the earth. I do not require it, for My perfection has paid that price. Remember? Give Me your listening ear, your open mind, your willing heart, and just see what I will do with them."

IN GOOD TIME

December 17   Matthew 12:34; 1 Corinthians 4:5

"All things in good time, My child. One step at a time as I have said so often before. All in My good time. We must always work from the inside out. When all is harmonious, balanced and at peace within—then the call of the outer self can be realized. But the inner work must be done first. I cannot work backwards. Do what you know to do **now**; then you will naturally know what to do **then**."

THE ARK OF SAFETY

December 18   Isaiah 43:1-3

"You ask for something to hang onto, as though you were trying to stay afloat in deep waters. Do you not know that you are already in the ark! The ark of safety. You only imagine that the swells of dark water swirl about you. It is not true. You are safe and secure, here in the ark of My love. You need only remember where you are."

ALL YOUR ANXIETY

December 19   1 Peter 5:7

" `Cast all your anxiety upon Him, for He cares for

you.' Does it say `part' of your anxiety? Read it over and over and over until it sinks down into your soul, down into the depths of your mind and spirit. How much anxiety are you to bear? If you are truly casting all of it upon Me, how much is left for you? Not a bit! Not an ounce of anxiety or worry or fear. Is not My provision a complete provision? And why do I do this for you? Why do I demand this relinquishment from you? Read it over and over—because I care for you."

THIS DAY

December 20   Proverbs 27:1

"One day at a time! Need I say more? How many times must I make this admonition? Will it ever be a reality in your life? Are you lacking this day, are your needs not met today? One day is enough to deal with. I will be there for every `today' that you live. But you must live them one at a time."

THE ADVOCATE

December 21   Job 16:19-21

"I go before the Father on your behalf each time that you choose to serve Him and not self. I present you to Him as a precious gift. I plead on your behalf for all the treasures of heaven to serve you that day. Treasures of wisdom and courage and faith and perseverance. The treasures of peace and rest and joy and love. The Father Himself gladly showers these blessings upon you as you walk with Me, as you take up your cross and follow Me."

GO FORWARD

December 22   Philippians 3:13-14

"Go forward without fear—that is always the banner

to be held high in the presence of all adversity, real or imagined. But remember I say, `Go forward, do not stand still!' It is always a forward march."

CONTROL THE MIND

December 23   1 Corinthians 2:11-16

"There must be control of the mind. Just as you control your body, so you must control your mind, your thoughts. Do you allow your body to run uncontrolled, moving wherever and in any manner it chooses? Of course not. So also bridle your thoughts and bring them into control. Direct them into channels of light, of godliness, of peace. The imagination is a powerful tool—use it for My glory and for your good. Choose also this day where your thoughts shall be!"

THE JUDGE

December 24   Matthew 7:1

"Answer Me this—who appointed you as judge over another? Does a judge not need to be appointed? I did not appoint you and who else has the power? None but Me. Does your judgment accomplish anything? Does it make anyone a better person? Does it then make you a better person? It does neither. It only tears down! Bring every thought to Me and to the obedience of Christ. Then judging will flee; self-pity will vanish—only joy and peace and trust will remain. Be intent only upon one thing—to glorify God and to be like Him. Cut the root of bitterness in your heart. Silence the voice of evil in your mind; push it all aside in one great sweep and once again, unhindered, follow Me."

VALLEYS OF PEACE

December 25   Galatians 5:22; Isaiah 26:3

"More and more let self sift through your fingertips and let My virtues fill you instead. This is My gift to you, My image fulfilled in you. This peace and rest in Me, no matter what is happening on the outside. This is My rest, promised in My Word. Obedience leads through valleys of peace."

GREAT GAIN

December 26   Romans 8:17

"The more of self you give up, the more of Me that you gain. You have found the secret, the key to vast treasure. Deny yourself and follow Me. Then all glory shall be yours, all that I have prepared for My followers belongs to you! I keep nothing from the obedient heart. All that belongs to Me belongs to you. Ask what you will—I am here to serve."

THE EYES OF FAITH

December 27   1 Peter 3:6

"Once again I must ask you, `Have I called you to fear? Have I called you to cowardice?' Of course I have not. Lift up your head, look about you, My child, with eyes of faith. All is not lost. There is much to be done. Many lessons to learn, many faults to correct, many bridges to span. I call you forward to do these tasks in My strength, with eternal hope, with grace and confidence as you follow Me."

DEADLY DISEASE

December 28   Phillipians 4:6

"Anxiety robs, it kills, it destroys—it turns life into ugly distortion in the eyes of man. It is Satan's tool, his pride and joy—to infect and infest the lives of My children with this deadly disease. The disease of unbelief called anxiety. Come to the great Physician—to be healed, to be counseled, to be set free."

OPPOSITION

December 29   Psalm 106:9-12

"Go your way, confident that the need will be met. When there is opposition, I am greater than any opposition. When there is a problem, I am always able to lead you out just as I lead the Israelites out of Egypt. Stand back and let Me do My work."

DISCIPLINE

December 30   Psalm 143:8

"I must remind you—discipline yourself to meet with Me each morning. Do not let Satan have the upper hand. He is so proud and sassy when he has won. Do not give him our victory—not even one time! Start each and every morning with Me, no matter what the cost or inconvenience. You will see such blessing for doing so. You and many others will reap the reward of your obedience."

LOOK TO ME

December 31   Ephesians 4:22-24

"As we end this year, let the old self, the old reactions

to life, be ended as well. Let us go on in newness of life, in new creation, in new strength and love, new faith and unruffled peace and calm. These are My New Year gifts to you. All this in unlimited abundance—abundance meant to fill your soul with joyful, joyful life. Let us leave the past and its failures, its outgrown attitudes and fears behind. Let us not look back! Look forward only, onward and upward. Look only to Me. This is My message to end the old year and to begin the new. This is always My message to you—simply, bravely, calmly **look to Me** in every circumstance, at every moment. Look, let go, and **LIVE!**"